Moments of
Comfort

Moments of Comfort

Embracing the Joy in Life's Simple Pleasures

Gill Hasson
Illustrated by Eliza Todd

CAPSTONE
A Wiley Brand

This edition first published 2022
© 2022 by Gill Hasson

Cover and interior layout/illustrations by Eliza Todd.

Registered office
John Wiley & Sons Ltd, The Atrium, Southern Gate, Chichester, West Sussex, PO19 8SQ,
United Kingdom

For details of our global editorial offices, for customer services and for information about
how to apply for permission to reuse the copyright material in this book please see our
website at www.wiley.com.

Wiley publishes in a variety of print and electronic formats and by print-on-demand. Some
material included with standard print versions of this book may not be included in e-books
or in print-on-demand. If this book refers to media such as a CD or DVD that is not included
in the version you purchased, you may download this material at http://booksupport.wiley.
com. For more information about Wiley products, visit www.wiley.com.

Designations used by companies to distinguish their products are often claimed as
trademarks. All brand names and product names used in this book are trade names, service
marks, trademarks or registered trademarks of their respective owners. The publisher is not
associated with any product or vendor mentioned in this book.

Limit of Liability/Disclaimer of Warranty: While the publisher and author have used their
best efforts in preparing this book, they make no representations or warranties with respect
to the accuracy or completeness of the contents of this book and specifically disclaim any
implied warranties of merchantability or fitness for a particular purpose. It is sold on the
understanding that the publisher is not engaged in rendering professional services and
neither the publisher nor the author shall be liable for damages arising herefrom. If professional advice or other expert assistance is required, the services of a competent professional
should be sought.

Library of Congress Cataloging-in-Publication Data
Names: Hasson, Gill, author.
Title: Moments of comfort : embracing the joy in life's simple pleasures / Gill Hasson.
Description: First edition. | Hoboken : Wiley, 2022.
Identifiers: LCCN 2021038691 (print) | LCCN 2021038692 (ebook) | ISBN 9780857089205
    (cloth) | ISBN 9780857089229 (adobe pdf) | ISBN 9780857089212 (epub)
Subjects: LCSH: Joy. | Motivation (Psychology) | Self-actualization (Psychology)
Classification: LCC BF575.H27 H3846 2022 (print) | LCC BF575.H27 (ebook) |
    DDC 152.4/2--dc23
LC record available at https://lccn.loc.gov/2021038691
LC ebook record available at https://lccn.loc.gov/2021038692

SKY0A4F656E-8CCC-4C7B-B7B8-88EFC4FA12B7_091621

This one is for you Hannah. xx

Contents

Introduction   x

Understanding Sadness   2
Accepting What Has Happened   4
Talking to Others   6
Finding the Good in Each Day   8
Coping with Being Unwell   10
Managing Worry and Anxiety   14
Getting Out in Nature   16
Taking the Pressure Off   18
Having Routines   20
Breathe in. Breathe out.   24
Seek Out and Appreciate Beauty   26
Asking For and Accepting Help   30
Bringing the Outside In   32
Spending Time Pottering   34
Dealing with Rudeness   36
The Tiny Frogs   38
Finding a Way to Forgive   40
Walking Meditations   42

Holidays and Short Breaks   44

Tea Ritual   46

Having the Right Words   48

Music and Song   50

Warming Comfort   52

Overcoming Loneliness   54

Spending Time with Your Dog   56

Finding Spirituality   58

Feeling Good About Yourself   60

Be Inspired by Other People   62

Having Patience   64

Gaining Perspective   66

To Everything, a Season   68

The Chinese Farmer's Tale   69

Reading Positive News   70

Managing Stress   72

Comforting Food   74

Five Senses Meditation   76

Indulging in Small Pleasures   78

Getting to Sleep   82

Reminiscing and Nostalgising   84

Laughing More   86

Finding Flow   88

Managing Disappointment   90

Accepting that All Things Come and Go   92

Beginning Again   94

Building Your Courage   96

Saying Affirmations   98

Being in Awe   102

The Power of Poetry   104

Creating Hope and Moving On   108

Easing Back into Life After an Illness   110

Managing Setbacks   112

Creating a Comfort Box   113

Journalling   114

Coping with Grief   116

Further Support and Advice   118

More Quotes for Comfort   120

My Notes   125

About the Author   139

About the Illustrator   141

Also by Gill Hasson   143

Introduction

'Cure sometimes, treat often, comfort always.' Hippocrates

Whether you're going through a tough time in your life or you're just feeling down – you've had a bad day, or it's been a long week – when life is difficult and you feel more like crying than carrying on, you need to do what you can to make things a bit easier and feel a little better.

Rather than struggle on thinking that you've got to pull your-self together and get on with it, it's important to know that it's OK not to be OK; it's OK to be sad and upset, to feel stressed, worried or anxious. It's important to know that what you need is kindness and some thoughtful attentions that will comfort you.

The good news is that you can provide that kindness and care for yourself. You don't have to make a big effort or make big changes; there are so many things that can bring you moments of comfort and small shots of joy. *Moments of Comfort* explains what they are and in what ways they can provide you with peace, encouragement and connection, strengthen and inspire you with hope.

Many of the subjects – such as gaining perspective and pa-tience, beginning again, getting out in nature, building courage and managing setbacks – I've written about before, in my books on mindfulness, positive thinking and emotional intelligence. I've included them in *Moments of Comfort* because the concepts of mindfulness, positive thinking etc. have such simple, sound advice for managing adversity; for navigating the difficulties and challenges in life.

Throughout this book, the advice is not to ignore, deny or suppress feelings such as sadness, disappointment, frustration and anger, but to take an acceptance and commitment approach. 'Acceptance and commitment' is a concept from mindfulness which suggests that you don't challenge or suppress thoughts and feelings that arise from adversity. Instead, you consciously notice and accept your thoughts and feelings. You accept that it's OK to think and feel whatever you think and feel. However, you don't get stuck in those thoughts and feelings; instead, sooner rather than later, you move on – you commit yourself – to more helpful thoughts and solutions.

If, for example, you'd had a bad day, you'd acknowledge the difficulties and the upset – maybe you'd rant and rave, maybe you'd tell someone else about it – but you wouldn't stay stuck in what happened. Instead, after a short while you'd move on and commit yourself to thinking about what you can do now – in the present – to lessen the upset, the stress or the pain.

An acceptance and commitment approach is effective because when you acknowledge and accept that things have been difficult, you let go of the emotional aspects and allow the rational, logical part of your mind to start working for you; to think in more helpful, positive ways. Ways that can bring you some comfort and a little bit of joy. It's a mindful approach because it emphasises that no matter what has happened there's always something positive that you can do now, in the present.

The songwriter and author Nick Cave has explained this well. In answer to a question on The Red Hand Files website (www. theredhandfiles.com) about how he perceives 'the utility of suffering' and how to bear it, he replied: 'We either transform our suffering into something else, or we hold on to it, and eventually pass it on ... To not transform our suffering compounds suffering.' Further on in his reply, Nick Cave suggests that we 'transform our suffering into kindness and compassion ... acting compassionately (is) an alchemical act that transforms pain into beauty. This is good. This is beautiful.'

It's true. We can't eradicate suffering, but we can learn to navigate it and eventually transform suffering so that there are some aspects that are positive; aspects that provide moments of comfort and sparks of joy.

UNDERSTANDING SADNESS

Whatever the difficulties or challenges and whatever the circumstances, when you've experienced something that leaves you feeling sad, upset, let down or disappointed, it helps to have a better understanding of those emotions.

It may be hard to believe, but feelings of sadness are there for a good reason; they actually have a positive intent. What's the positive intent? It's to slow down your mind and body to give you time to take in your new circumstances and accept that what has happened has happened. And that nothing can change that. Acknowledge your sadness. Tell yourself that you have every right to feel upset. Berating yourself for feeling upset just creates an additional burden.

It is OK to be sad and upset. You might think, 'I shouldn't be so upset. What's wrong with me?' There's nothing wrong with you. You simply need to accept sadness for what it is; a temporary and useful state that can help you adjust – to get used to changed, different circumstances – and to accommodate the changes and learn to live with them.

Whether you've been let down or disappointed or you've suffered a loss or major life change, be kind to yourself; don't expect too much of yourself, your mind needs time to catch up with and process the changes in you life; your new reality.

ACCEPTING WHAT HAS HAPPENED

'Acceptance doesn't mean resignation; it means understanding that something is what it is and there's got to be a way through it.'
– Michael J Fox

Acceptance means understanding that something has or has not happened. Acceptance means understanding that you cannot change what has or hasn't already happened. Right now, something is what it is. What could be more futile than resisting what already is?

Acceptance doesn't mean you have to resign yourself to something; to give in. It doesn't mean you can't do anything about what's happened, but before you do, you need to accept what has brought you to this point; to this present moment.

In fact, in what's known as the 'acceptance paradox', acceptance is what makes change possible. If you don't acknowledge and accept what has happened, it's difficult to move on from that point. But once you do accept something, rather than react to it – take impulsive, opposing action – you can respond to it; act thoughtfully and favourably.

So do remember that when you stop dwelling on what could, should or shouldn't have happened, you free your mind to be able to focus on what to do next.

'God, grant me the serenity to accept the things I cannot change, courage to change the things I can, and wisdom to know the difference.' – Reinhold Niebuhr

Whatever it is – you've lost your job, a relationship has ended or you're unwell – acknowledge what has happened. You can acknowledge it by saying it in your head or you can say it out loud; describe what has happened. You might find it helpful to write down what's happened.

Acknowledge your feelings too. It's not helpful to resist, deny, ignore or suppress your feelings about what's happened. Allow yourself to feel upset, disappointed, frustrated or angry. Cry if you feel like it. Crying is cathartic; it helps relieve emotional tension. It unifies your thoughts, feelings and physical body.

Give yourself time but don't get stuck in resenting what happened and railing about it. Know that rumination – going over and over your feelings of sadness and disappointment or frustration and anger – can't go on for ever. With acceptance, you don't hold on to thoughts, feelings, situations and events. You understand that they are part of the past. At some point you need to let go and move on. And sometimes, that might be in a different direction.

TALKING TO OTHERS

You might feel as if few people, if any, understand what you're going through. Often, other people don't know what to do or say so they do or say nothing. So even though you're the one who's facing a tough time you may need to be the one to get in touch.

Reach out to others; a friend or family member who will have a calm concern and will listen and comfort you. If you know someone you can talk to who won't try to judge or fix you, tell them what's happened and how you've been feeling: confused? Anxious? Sad? Angry and upset? Perhaps you've been feeling overwhelmed or exhausted?

You might find that some friends or family members can't handle your feelings. That's OK. Everyone has their abilities and their limits. If someone isn't able to listen or talk with you about how you're feeling, ask them to do something practical to help. Leave talking about how you feel to someone who is able to listen and talk with you about it.

You may want to talk to someone you know who's experienced the same difficulties. But if you don't know of anyone who's gone through the same experience, Google a relevant support group or helpline. You'll be able to talk to people who understand what you are or have been going through, provide opportunities to share experiences with others who have been or are going through the same thing and get information and ideas on how to cope, to move on or feel better.

You can still reach out for support even if you are feeling a little sad

FINDING THE GOOD IN EACH DAY

'Be thankful for what you have and you will end up with more.'
– Oprah Winfrey

When life feels like it's weighing you down, it can feel like everything is wrong, bad or hopeless; there's nothing positive. But even during the worst of times, there can be something to be thankful for. Every day, there is something positive and good. Most of the time it's not obvious. You have to look and often you have to look hard. You have to tap into gratitude.

Gratitude involves being aware of and acknowledging the positive things in your life right now. Even if you get to the end of the day feeling that not much went right, gratitude helps you see life through a more positive lens. Just pausing to identify what you're thankful for can have a positive impact; when you focus your attention on the positive things, events and people in your life each day, you encourage your own happiness and wellbeing.

The smallest things can make the biggest difference. Gratitude happens best when you make an effort to acknowledge the things that often go unnoticed or unappreciated. It helps create a more balanced perspective.

At the end of each day, identify and reflect on three positive things that happened in your day. It needs only to be the small things – it could simply be that you had something delicious to eat, that the sun shone, or that you received a supportive message from someone. Maybe you enjoyed the sound of the rain on your windows this evening. It could be that you managed to fix something, a cupboard door or undo a knot in a shoelace. Maybe you dropped your phone, thought the screen had smashed but then realised it hadn't.

Writing in the *Guardian* in November 2020, journalist Kathryn Bromwich described how starting six years previously, she'd been writing down three good things that happened in her day, every day. 'It doesn't matter how big or small they are. It could be having pastries in bed. Spotting a fox in the garden. Successfully descaling a kettle ... I have found it vital ... to focus on the things that have gone right. Left unattended, my thoughts have a tendency to slip into a downward spiral.'

Even if you have a bad day, at the end of the day, like Kathryn, find three good things that happened. You could write them down in a notebook, or you may simply reflect on what those things are while you are brushing your teeth. Appreciate just knowing that you had good in your day so that, whatever else happened, whatever difficulties you experienced, you know that there was some positivity there.

Just make an effort for a couple of weeks to identify the good things – the small joys – in your day. After a while, identifying and reflecting on the small pleasures will become a habit. A comforting, joyful habit.

COPING WITH BEING UNWELL

None of us choose to get injured or be ill. But to a certain extent, we can choose how we deal with it. Having an injury or being unwell – physically or mentally – is the time to prioritise selfcare; to be gentle and easy with yourself, so don't pressure yourself to carry on as normal. If you work, call in sick. If you have social plans, cancel or reschedule. If there's housework to do, leave it. Rest is more important. Feel guilty? It's misplaced guilt; you're not doing anything wrong by doing what you can to get better. Time and energy you put into other things is time and energy diverted from you getting better. Your health is important and in the long run you will be able to do more if you rest now, as it will speed up your recovery.

Any day that you're unwell, make sure you're comfortable. Wear comfy, loose clothes, curl up in bed or bring your duvet and pillows into the living room and make yourself comfortable on the sofa. Gather everything you need – medication, tissues, books and magazines, laptop and phone and their chargers, the TV remote and anything else you may need or want – into one place so you don't have to keep expending energy and effort getting up and down.

Being unwell is a time to do things that bring comfort and calm. All of the little pleasures that you usually don't find time for can be enjoyed when you're unwell. There's nothing to feel guilty about – you're not doing anything wrong by indulging yourself in this way. Quite the opposite – you're doing everything right; you're taking care of yourself so that you can get better.

Eat healthily but do also eat comfort food. (See page 74.) Don't let food shopping sap your energy. Try to plan for food items and meals you're likely to need for the next few days and either ask someone else to get it or do an online food order.

If you have children to take care of, know that you can't be Supermum or Superdad while you're feeling ill. Your children certainly won't hold it against you forever if you ditch the sports practice, craft activities and outdoor adventures for a few days and let them resort to the TV and computer games. Will they? Give yourself – and them – a break.

And in the evening, when the children go to bed, if you're not already there, go to bed too. Don't use the evenings to get other stuff done. Your body imposes a curfew when you're ill – obey it or it will punish you the next day!

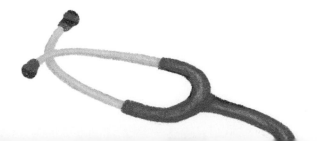

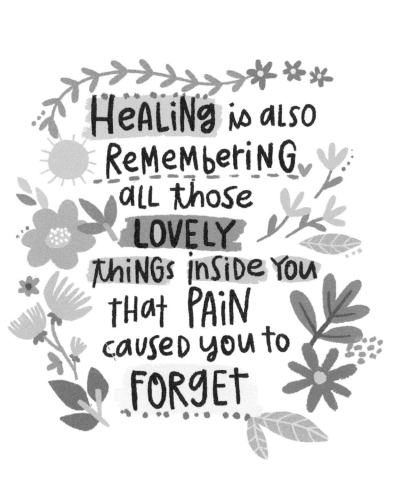

HEALiNG is also ReMeMberiNG all those LOVELY things inside You that PAIN caused you to FORGET

MANAGING WORRY AND ANXIETY

'Worrying is using your imagination to create something you don't want.' – Abraham Hicks

We all know what it's like to experience worry and anxiety; to be concerned about an upcoming medical test for example, or an interview or exam. Maybe you're worried about making a journey, attending a social event, starting a new job or university? Perhaps you have financial worries or you're anxious about your health.

Whenever you are worried or anxious and whatever it's about, you may think that you've no control over how events could turn out and how you'll cope if things do go wrong. Maybe your stomach gets in knots or you feel nauseous. Perhaps you find it difficult to concentrate; negative thoughts dominate your mind.

Like all emotions, worry and anxiety do have a positive intent; they serve as your internal alarm and prompt you to do what you can to manage or prevent the worst case scenario from happening.

So, recognising that you're worried is a good thing when it spurs you to take helpful, constructive action. But too often, worries and anxious thoughts drag you out of the present moment and into an unknown future, allowing unrelenting doubts and fears and negative possibilities to overwhelm your mind and paralyse you. But getting stuck in worry and anxiety doesn't help you think clearly and allow you to come up with constructive ways to deal with a potential problem and improve a situation.

A mindful approach can help you focus on what you can do in the present moment, rather than be pre-living the future.

'Don't worry about the future; or worry, but know that worrying is as effective as trying to solve an algebra equation by chewing bubblegum.' – Mary Schmich

Start by identifying what you're actually worried about. What's the worst that can happen? Write it down. Next, identify possible solutions. Write those ideas down. Once you start looking for solutions and doing something about the problem, you may feel less worried because you are thinking and acting in the present rather than projecting yourself into the future.

After you've decided on a solution – a plan for what to do if the worst did happen, decide what you need to do next. What's the first step? Take that first step.

Now that you have a solution and a plan, if you find yourself worrying tell yourself, 'Stop! I have a plan!' and keep your thoughts on that. Visualise a positive outcome; create images for yourself where you see yourself coping and things turning out well.

Then, turn to something else. Identify activities that you can turn to when you want to switch off from worrying; something that you can dip into for ten minutes or immerse yourself in for an hour. Something that brings your attention to the present and keeps you focused and engaged. It could be listening to music, reading a book, watching a film, doing a puzzle – a crossword or sudoku – a computer game, yoga, a game of tennis. It could be work, housework, time with friends. Anything that makes it difficult for worrying thoughts to find their way into your head.

GETTING OUT IN NATURE

Nature is both permanent and ever-changing. Whenever you can, try and spend some time of your day or your week in nature. Most of us have somewhere near to the natural world, even if it's only a small park or garden. With more than 62,000 urban green spaces in Great Britain, one should never be too far away. The Wildlife Trusts, www.wildlifetrusts.org, has a searchable online map of its nature reserves, almost all of which have free entry; it also provides a list of accessible nature reserves. And Ordnance Survey's Greenspace – getoutside. ordnancesurvey.co.uk/greenspaces/ – shows thousands of green spaces for leisure and recreation.

Get to know a tree. Trees, like us, live through the cycles of change that come with the changing seasons. Trees bend with the winds, stand strong in the storms, and yet they continue to grow upward. Trees remind us that our existence also involves change and transformation. Look in your garden, your local park, down the street, in a field, a wood or a forest for a tree that you could get to know. Be aware of how a tree changes throughout the seasons. Not sure what tree it is? The Woodland Trust, woodlandtrust.org.uk, have a tree identification app.

Try forest bathing. Forest bathing is spending time in woods or forests to connect with nature to promote a sense of wellbeing. With forest bathing, as you walk, you take the time to take in the natural surroundings; the rays of sunlight, raindrops catching the leaves, the smells of the damp earth, the sounds of birdsong and so on.

Visit a city farm. If you live in a town or city, visit a local community or city farm. Social Farms & Gardens is a UK-wide charity supporting communities to farm, garden and grow together. Their website farmgarden.org.uk/ has information about visiting and opportunities to get involved in anything from small fruit and veg plots on urban housing estates to large-scale rural care farms.

Take an alpaca for a walk. Alpacas are delightful and friendly animals; they are gentle, easy to handle and relaxing to be around. Alpaca walking is on offer all over the UK. The experience typically involves a training session on how to behave around alpacas, leading them on a halter for about an hour and then feeding them. The British Alpaca Society, www.bas-uk.com/, can tell you where to find alpaca farms that offer alpaca walks and treks near you. Or Google 'alpaca walking' in your area.

Watch the birds. You don't need any special equipment. Hang a bird feeder outside a window. If there's space, you could build a small wooden nesting box on a tree or under a windowsill. See the RSPB website, rspb.org.uk, for more information on feeding, sheltering and watching birds.

17

TAKING THE PRESSURE OFF

When you're going through difficulties in your life, you need to take the pressure off; let go of some of your commitments, duties and obligations so that you don't get overwhelmed. You don't have to cope brilliantly and you don't have to be amazing; you just need to do the minimum to get by, because that's all you can do and for now, that's just how it's going to be.

Give yourself some time to think about which of your commitments and obligations are not so important right now.

Ask yourself questions such as:

- What do I want to do with my time?

- For now, what do I have to do and not have to do?

- Where do I want to go and not go?

- Who do I want to see and not want to see?

- Who depends on me – who do I have to see or attend to?

- For now, what can I stop doing and who can I stop seeing?

Cutting back on commitments doesn't mean that you should remove yourself from everything and everyone, but when you're experiencing difficulties in your life you do need to be aware of your limits and know that it's OK to stick to them; saying 'no thanks' or 'not now' to requests for your time; for your presence, abilities and contributions.

It is OK to say no. It's not selfish or unkind. When someone asks you to do something, makes a suggestion or extends a well-meaning invitation notice how you immediately feel. Uninterested? Anxious? Pressured? Stressed? Simply say, 'Thank you for asking me, but I don't want to / can't / don't feel up to it / not this time.'

There's no need for a long explanation and excuses. Be honest. You only need one valid reason why you can't or don't want to do something.

Although you may need to step back from life for a while when you're going through a difficult period, don't drop all your connections with others. Your link to family and friends is important for your sense of wellbeing and belonging. You just need to tighten the circle for a bit and limit your time to spending it with those people who support or comfort you in some way.

HAVING ROUTINES

If things happen that upend your life and your world changes, if you're facing uncertainty and feeling unsure, routines can provide some reassurance and stability.

When you have activities, tasks or chores that are routine, if other things in your life are uncertain or out of your control, routines provide an anchor of predictability. Rather than spending time and energy worrying about situations that are out of your hands, routines bring you back to the things that are in your control.

The simplest of things – the times of day you get up, shower, eat a meal, feed your cat, watch the news in the evening, go to bed – create a sense of safety and purpose and give you something real to hold onto.

As well as creating a structure to your day, routines make little in the way of demands; they simplify your life. You've done them so often, in the same way and with such regularity, that whatever else is or isn't happening for you, you do get some things done without having to think about them too much.

There's comfort in sameness and familiarity. So when aspects of your life are uncertain and you're unsettled, identify and hold on to what's unchanging. On the next two pages, write down the things – the daily or weekly activities – that are routine. Having some things in your life – walking the dog every day, the school run, the time you watch a TV programme, a weekly supermarket shop, going for a run at weekends, visiting a family member – is a reminder that some things are still the same.

even in the
unceRtainty
the STARS
still SHiNe
the SUN still
Rises

MY ROUTINES

Things I do on a daily basis:

....

....

....

....

....

....

....

....

....

....

....

....

....

....

Things I do on **a weekly basis:**

....

....

....

....

....

....

....

....

....

....

....

....

....

....

....

BREATHE IN. BREATHE OUT.

'When you own your breath, nobody can steal your peace.' – Author unknown

In mindfulness practice, breathing provides a focal point for your mind that can help slow everything down, calm your mind and your body and bring you into the present moment.

Mindful breathing is like a reset button that you can push to return yourself to the present moment whenever you feel the need; an effective way of orienting yourself to the now, not because the breath has some magical property, but because it's always there with you.

Being aware of your breathing is a simple thing you can do anywhere, any time, to anchor you to the moment. Just bring your awareness to breathing in ... then breathing out. That's mindful breathing.

There are, though, a number of ways that you can use your mind or body to keep focused on breathing. Try them out and see which one you prefer; which ones are the most doable for you. Which breathing technique you use is not as important as just remembering to use one of them!

So, the next time you find yourself overwhelmed, say to yourself, 'Be here, now.' Pause. And breathe. Just take a few minutes to stop what you're doing and do nothing. Just focus on breathing. A simple two-minute breathing space will help calm you down, re-engage your brain and allow you to collect and clarify your thoughts.

Feel your breathing. Place one hand on your chest and feel your breath moving into and out of your body. Notice the natural rhythm. Be aware of the coolness of the air as you breathe in and the warmth of the air leaving you as you exhale.

Breathe slowly and deeply. Start by breathing normally, then, every few breaths, inhale through your nose slowly to a count of five. Pause and hold your breath for a count of three then breathe out slowly, blowing out air through your mouth. When you've exhaled completely, take two breaths in your normal rhythm, and then repeat the cycle.

Use your imagination. Breathe in like you're smelling the scent of a flower. Breathe out like you're blowing bubbles. Or, imagine breathing out to the ends of the universe and breathing from there back into your body. Or, breathe colour; imagine the colour of the air filling not just your lungs but your entire body.

Count backwards. Inhale deeply. When you breathe out, count backwards from nine; nine, eight, seven, six and so on. On the next breath, when you breathe out, count backwards from eight. With the next breath, count backwards from seven. And so on, adjusting the length of time you breathe in and out according to which number you are counting backwards from.

SEEK OUT AND APPRECIATE BEAUTY

'I don't think of all the misery, but of the beauty that still remains.'
– Anne Frank

Beauty; it's the quality or combination of qualities present in something or someone that pleases the aesthetic senses, especially the sight. Beauty can be found in shapes and colours, designs and patterns. It can be found in a view – a landscape, a cityscape or a seascape. Beauty can be found in art and architecture, a poem, a painting, a person, a face. Beauty can be found in a sound – music and song, the wind and rain.

Why does an appreciation of beauty matter? It matters because beauty can give you a sense of calm and peace. Beauty is uplifting and inspiring.

Beauty is, of course, in the eye of the beholder. What do you perceive to be beautiful? What sights and sounds, tastes and smells please you? Consciously look for and appreciate instances of the beauty of what we are naturally a part of, concepts such as: music and art, wildlife and the miracles of nature. You can write down your 'instances of beauty' as and when you come across them, on the next two pages.

Although you can admire and enjoy beauty without feeling a need to do anything about it, you could start a collection of photos of things you find beautiful – anything from a view or a sunset to the details of a flower, a shell or a feather – to gaze at whenever you need a lift.

breathe
in BEAUTY
breathe
OUT JOY

INSTANCES OF BEAUTY

....

....

....

....

....

....

....

....

....

....

....

....

....

....

....

....

Asking for and accepting help

'I get by with a little help from my friends.' – Lennon and McCartney

Let others know when you're struggling. Don't be boring and go on about it but don't say you're fine when you're not. Don't say you don't want to be any trouble. Don't be a banana! Take help when it's offered. And if someone says 'let me know if I can do anything', think of something!

If they don't offer, then ask. Ask for help and support. Be specific about what it is that you'd like someone to do for you and ask them. Whether it's getting the washing off the line, cooking dinner, walking the dog every day, making some phone calls on your behalf or just keeping you company for a while, let others help.

Make it easy for them to help you. Be direct – don't drop hints, sigh or look sad. Clearly explain what you need help with. Don't waffle or apologise for needing help. Don't say 'I know you're really busy, so only if you have time … only if you want to … sorry, I know this is a lot to ask …' Instead, simply say 'I need help with ……… . Would you be able to ……… today/tomorrow/at the weekend for me?' This way, the person is clear about what, how and when to help you.

Just as going through a tough time is an opportunity to do things that bring you comfort, it's also a time to ask for and accept the care and help of others. So if someone you trust is happy to help, just let them.

Sure, asking for help requires surrendering control to someone else. But even if they don't do things exactly how you'd want them, let go of perfection and accept that for now, how and what they're doing is good enough.

Maybe, though, you're worried that your request for help will be rejected and you'll feel embarrassed for having asked. Perhaps you think you should be able to cope, that your situation isn't as bad as some people's.

Maybe you don't want to appear needy or for anyone to see that you're struggling; you want people to think that you're in control and can handle things.

But you get in your own way when you make asking for help mean something negative about you when it doesn't. Asking for or accepting help doesn't mean you're inadequate, it simply means you need help, support and advice with a specific issue for a time. Asking for help shows that you know that trying to do everything yourself can leave you feeling overwhelmed and stressed and would probably set you back.

Even if the person you ask can't help you, they may have some suggestions as to how best to cope or who else might be able to help you. Whoever and whatever it is other people are able to do for you, do tell them you appreciate their concern or support!

BRINGING THE OUTSIDE IN

'Plants give us oxygen for the lungs and for the soul.' – Linda Solegato

Indoor plants are living, growing, changing things that can provide you with a connection to nature. Whether you work at the top of a skyscraper or you live in a tiny studio apartment, you can have your own garden indoors with plants in pots, boxes or hanging containers.

Houseplants come in a range of sizes from tiny to huge. Some have architecturally stunning shapes to their form and foliage, others have beautiful blooms in every colour.

According to a study published in 2015 in the *Journal of Physiological Anthropology*, 'active interaction' with indoor plants – touching and watering for example – can have a calming and soothing effect. In fact, just being in close proximity to plants can help you feel calm and heal faster from injuries. A Kansas State University study, published in 2009, recommended indoor plants as a 'noninvasive, inexpensive, and effective complementary medicine for surgical patients'.

But maybe you've stayed away from keeping a houseplant because you think it requires some sort of special skill or knowledge to keep it alive. Not so. You just need to meet a plant's basic needs – the right amount of light, temperature and water – and then do what is known in Taoism as 'wuwei'. Wu wei is a state of being in which our actions and inaction are effortlessly in alignment with the ebb and flow of the elemental cycles of the natural world. Wuwei involves doing nothing; not trying to make something happen, just going with the flow, letting things be and take their own course.

'Watching something grow is good for morale. It helps us believe in life.' – Myron Kaufmann

Start with plants that are easy to care for. English ivy is known to grow effortlessly. Spider plants are low maintenance houseplants; they aren't too fussy about light, temperature or water. Peace lilies have elegant curving white blooms and dark leaves and are easy to grow. A pothos plant will grow quickly from a pot or trailing from a hanging basket with minimal care.

Succulents and cacti are slow-growing and need little care and attention. They do best with bright light, well-drained pots and little water. (They store what water they do get, allowing them to survive droughts.) There are dozens of varieties to choose from; each very distinct in appearance and in the right place, these are plants that truly thrive on neglect.

Look for signs of new growth in your plants. Look at how your plant develops new leaves; each plant has its own specific way of producing new growth. Prayer plant leaves, for example, emerge from the stem in a loose roll that elegantly unfurls. Spider plants produce baby plants at the end of long tendrils that can be plucked off and planted.

Grow your own; grow an avocado plant. Growing an avocado plant indoors is simple. It won't bear fruit, but you'll have a new houseplant for free. Just Google 'Grow an avocado seed' to find out how.

SPENDING TIME POTTERING

Although other people can be a source of practical support, advice, empathy and sympathy, often there's comfort and joy to be found in spending time alone; time in solitude.

As well as giving you time to focus on interests and hobbies, solitude gives you time and space to think – to reflect and plan, to process experience. Solitude can also be time not to think; it can be time spent pottering.

When you're pottering – whether it's in your home or garden – you're going contentedly from one simple easy-to-achieve task to the next. You're occupied, but not with anything especially demanding. You don't have to plan, put much effort in, be good at it or do it well.

Of course, one person's pottering may be another person's unwanted chore – dusting, ironing, a minor repair, emptying the dishwasher, tidying the kitchen – are routine activities that we usually just want to get done and out of the way. But while pottering results in something getting done – something gets cleaned or sorted, made or mended – it's the unhurried, relaxed approach that occurs during pottering that's beneficial to our wellbeing.

down time

REST & RESTORE

'Don't underestimate the value of Doing Nothing, of just going along, listening to all the things you can't hear, and not bothering.'
– Winnie the Pooh. (A. A. Milne)

Sorting through the contents of drawers, rearranging cupboards, sorting things into piles, arranging books and objects on a shelf are all examples of pottering. So are watering plants, pruning and dead heading. None of these things is strictly necessary, but doing them gives you a sense of control and satisfaction with what you're doing and how you're doing it.

Pottering activities have a uniquely restful and restorative effect; a key aspect of pottering is the slow pace at which you do it; you're unhurried, free of stress and responsibility. And although you don't have to think much about what you're doing, pottering activities free your mind to order your thoughts and think through aspects of your life.

Whether it's half an hour, an hour or a whole morning, with unstructured downtime doing something that is slightly useful you are engaged in the gentlest of ways. The outcome of this is that your mind is rested and you are relaxed.

There's no pressure with pottering; nothing has to be completed; you can always pick it up tomorrow where you left off.

DEALING WITH RUDENESS

'To penetrate the hardest armour, use the softest touch.' – Haven Trevino

A few years ago, writer and teacher Arthur Rosenfield was in a 'drive-thru' queue at a Starbucks in Florida. The man in the car behind him was getting impatient and angry, leaning on his horn and shouting insults at both Arthur and the Starbucks workers.

Arthur looked in the rear view mirror. The face of the impatient driver behind him was twisted with anger and hate. 'I'll show you what happens to rude and impatient people,' thought Arthur. But then he caught himself; he refocused his eyes and noticed that his own face didn't look much different.

In one moment Arthur had what he calls a 'change of consciousness'; he chose to keep calm and change the negativity into something positive. Arthur paid for both his own coffee and the other man's order and then he went on his way. When he got home at the end of the day, Arthur discovered that his actions had featured on NBC News. Within 24 hours they had spread around the world on the internet.

No doubt you too have met mean, rude people; you're going about your day, when out of the blue, someone pulls their car abruptly in front of you, or they jump the queue. Perhaps they interrupt you repeatedly when you're talking, say or write something horrible to deliberately hurt your feelings.

Usually, when others are rude or hostile, we jump at the chance to assume the worst and defend or attack. How can you – like Arthur Rosenfield – have a 'change of consciousness'. How do you reach inside and pull out kindness when it's the farthest thing from your mind?

'Silence the angry man with love. Silence the ill-natured man with kindness. Silence the miser with generosity. Silence the liar with truth.' – Buddha

Practise responding with kindness. Next time you read or listen (on the radio, TV or overhear in public) to someone else's opinion and it really annoys you, think about giving them the benefit of the doubt. Believe something good about someone, rather than something bad.

Suspend judgement. Assume that the other person might have had a difficult day and that unfortunately they're taking it out on you. Try to keep an overall positive impression of others, and keep their negative qualities in the larger context of their good and bad nature. With this perspective you will be in a much better position to respond with positivity.

Next time someone is mean or rude to you, breathe. Count backwards, from seven. Be aware of how you react; notice that your body has tensed and your mind is attempting to assign meaning and blame.

Know when to let it go. If you can make an appropriate, kind gesture to the other person, go ahead. But if they reject it or if the person is someone you don't know, walk away. Maya Angelou once said 'When someone shows you who they are, believe them the first time.' The last thing you want is to get yourself into trouble. People who are mean and rude are stressed out and can flip at any time. Do or say one wrong thing and you could end up in trouble.

THE TINY FROGS

Once upon a time, there was a group of tiny frogs who arranged a competition. The aim was to reach the top of a tower.

A huge crowd of frogs gathered to watch the race and cheer on the contestants. The race began.

None of the frogs watching in the crowd believed that the contestants would reach to the top. After all, it was a very tall tower. The crowd grew and many yelled,

'Oh, that is way too difficult!!'
'They will never make it to the top!'
'It's impossible! The tower is too high!'

One by one, the tiny frogs collapsed and fell off the tower. Still, there was a group of determined frogs that climbed higher and higher. But the crowd continued to yell,

'It is too difficult! No one will make it!'

Discouraged and convinced by the negative cries, more of these tiny frogs collapsed and fell off the tower. Other frogs who were still climbing eventually lost strength and, exhausted, gave up.

By now, all the other tiny frogs had either collapsed or given up, except for that one tiny frog. This one tiny frog persisted. He climbed. And he climbed. And he climbed. He pushed on. How, though? How is he able to climb so far when others are failing? the crowd wondered. They continued to yell, directing their cries at the one tiny frog:

'It's too difficult!!'
'You'll never make it to the top!!'
'Stop now – before you fall!'

But the tiny frog persisted and he climbed further, seemingly undaunted. Finally, he reached the top of the tower. He had reached his destination!

All the tiny frogs were amazed how this one frog was **able to** make it to the top. They crowded around him, wanting to know his secret.

As it turned out, he was deaf.

When you are struggling to achieve something, like the tiny frog, be deaf to the naysayers!

FINDING A WAY TO FORGIVE

'When you forgive, you in no way change the past, but you sure do change the future.' – Bernard Meltzer

Have you been let down by someone else? Maybe someone – a friend, colleague or family member – betrayed your trust? Perhaps a stranger caused a major difficulty in your life? Whoever and whatever it was that happened, after your initial disappointment, shock or anger has passed, you're presented with a new challenge; do you forgive the person?

Forgiveness means letting go of the resentment, frustration or anger that you feel as a result of someone else's actions. It involves no longer wanting punishment, revenge or compensation. It means recognising that you have already been hurt once, so you don't need to let the offence, the hurt and pain keep hurting and distressing you by holding onto it.

All the time you feel unable to forgive, you're holding on to something that happened days, weeks, months or even years ago. But forgiveness is first and foremost for your benefit – for your peace of mind – not the person who hurt or offended you. Not forgiving is like deliberately keeping a wound open; it remains raw and it festers. On the other hand, when you forgive, you allow yourself to heal.

Of course, forgiveness isn't easy when you're disappointed or angry, filled with thoughts of retribution or revenge. It can also be hard to forgive if you don't know how to resolve a situation. But if you've now reached a point where you **want to put** someone else's actions behind you and **move on with your life,** there are a number of steps you can take.

Accept what has happened and let go. No doubt the other person is responsible for their actions and you wish that what they did had never happened. But you can't change what has already happened. Instead of thinking about retribution, think about what you learned from the experience. Is there anything you would do differently to avoid becoming involved in a similar situation?

Identify and focus on the positive aspects. Maybe other people were helpful and supportive when you suffered a wrong by someone else? Maybe, if you've now cut this person from your life, you realise how much better off you are without them? Whatever the positive aspects, keep your mind focused on them.

Change the story you replay to yourself and to other people. Each time you think about what happened, each time you tell the story from the past you relive it in the present. Change your story to one that tells of your decision to forgive; to accept and learn from what happened, to identify any positive aspects and move on.

Write about it. You might find it helpful to write an honest, emotional letter telling the other person how hurt and angry you are. Then tear it up and burn it. As you watch the smoke rise, imagine it carrying your hurt and disappointment into the air; let it go.

Be patient. Give yourself time to heal. Know that letting go, acceptance and forgiveness are all part of a process. Sometimes your ability to forgive will come quickly and easily. At other times it will take longer.

WALKING MEDITATIONS

'Quiet the mind, and the soul will speak.' – Ma Jaya Sati Bhagavati

What does it mean to meditate? Meditation is a period of time devoted to letting go of thoughts about the past and the future; experiencing each moment as a new beginning; accepting and engaging with the moment; being without judgement. Meditation focuses, quietens and calms the mind. Meditation connects your mind, body and spirit.

But what if you find it difficult to sit still for any length of time? You can try a walking meditiation. A walking meditation offers an alternative for those who struggle with sitting meditation but still seek the benefits.

A walking meditation is a meditation in movement. Unlike a sitting meditation, with a walking meditation, you're not completely disengaging from the outside world; for one thing you keep your eyes open during walking meditation!

A walking meditation uses the movements of walking as the focus; you keep your awareness involved with the experience of walking; experiencing the simplicity and peace of being with one step at a time, with nothing else to do and nowhere to go.

Try a simple walking meditation: walking back and forth, along the same path. Choose a path – indoors or outside – with a start point and an end point. A path of about 10 to 20 metres long is good but you may want to experiment with paths of different lengths and find one that works well for you. You practise meditation by walking between these two points, being mindful of each step, and bringing your attention to the rhythm of the walk.

As you walk, look down along the path about two metres ahead, to ensure that you remain on the path and know when to turn around. Each time you come to the end of the path, as you turn, be aware of where your mind is at. If it has wandered, bring it back to the here and now.

Continue to pace up and down for the duration of the meditation period; for as little as 5 minutes or maybe up to ten or twenty minutes or more. If it helps, chant a mantra – particular words or phrases – to help you maintain focus and keep your mind clear of other thoughts.

Try a walking and breathing meditation. This involves focusing on your breathing as you walk. Breathe in for 3, 4, or 5 steps. Breathe out for the same number of steps. A variation of this is, right after breathing in, to hold your breath for the same number of steps before you breathe out. Another variation is to exhale for twice as long as you inhale. So, inhale for a count of 4 steps, exhale for a count of 8 steps.

HOLIDAYS AND SHORT BREAKS

'A vacation is what you take when you can no longer take what you've been taking.' – Earl Wilson

It's good to step back and switch off from the stresses and strains of home and work life, but is a long holiday – a couple of weeks or more – best, or would a short break be just as good?

Either. The benefits of short breaks – a break from everyday life, new experiences and perspectives and making new memories – can last for just as long as a week or two away. What's important is not how long the break is, more that you go somewhere different; that your time away is different from everyday life and is enjoyable.

Short breaks – three or four days – can, for some of us, be easier to fit into our lives. For others, a good long break may be what we prefer. Either way, the process of planning a break or holiday and then looking forward to it is also part of the pleasure. What do you enjoy? You might like spending your time walking in the country. Perhaps you prefer to be lounging round a pool, lying on the beach or sitting in a cosy cottage, reading a book by a roaring fire.

Perhaps you could plan a short break around an event in another town or city such as a concert, a show, an exhibition or sports event. What about an active weekend away – an adventure such as bushcraft or a survival weekend – or learning a creative skill, an art or craft?

Holidays don't have to cost much; how about a house swap with a friend or family member who lives in another part of the country? Or go to www.lovehomeswap.com/

A working holiday can give you a whole new perspective on life; www.workaway.info/ lists opportunities for anyone who wants to give back to the communities and places they visit.

If you have a pet, there's probably a friend or neighbour who could take care of them if you're going away for a short break. Or go to a pet-sitting service such as www.homesitters.co.uk/ (You might even consider becoming a house sitter yourself!)

The people you are with are as much a contributor to a good holiday as where you go and what you do. Choose wisely! You might go with family or friends or on your own; search online for holiday companies specifically for single travellers. You'll also find that a range of holiday companies that organise group holidays welcome people with their partners or on their own; that all are made to feel welcome and included.

Finally, do take into account the day before and the day after your holiday. Maybe start or end your holiday a day early rather than screeching around until the 11th hour the day before the holiday starts or arriving home and hitting the ground running.

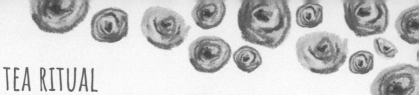

TEA RITUAL

If you enjoy drinking tea, then making tea will be something you have done many many times. It's a simple familiar process for you.

Like all rituals, the ritual of making and drinking tea – the succession of simple actions carried out in a specific sequence – can help to slow you down, connect you to yourself, to where you are, to the here and now.

So when things become uncertain or you're unsure about something, pause and make tea.

You might store your tea in a lovely container. Perhaps you have a special teapot, one handed down from a parent or grandparent that you could use for your tea ritual. Try using loose leaf tea; smell the aroma of the tea leaves, use your fingers to put in the tea leaves and feel their size, shape and texture as you drop the tea into a warmed teapot. Listen to the water – the bubbling and gurgling – as it begins to boil. Watch for the wisps of steam coming from the spout. Listen to the sound of the water pouring into the pot or the cup. Be aware of the change in the colour of the water – the transformation from clear water to tea – as it's poured onto the tea leaves. What aromas rise up in the steam? Are they earthy, floral or fruity? If you add milk, watch the colour change again.

Take a sip of tea. Sit calmly and quietly as you drink the tea. Now and again, make a ritual out of making tea. It can slow you down and connect you to the moment. And all with just some water and leaves.

A CUP OF

HEALING

HAVING THE RIGHT WORDS

*'Emotions, in my experience, aren't covered by single words.
I don't believe in "sadness," "joy," or "regret." … the language …
oversimplifies feeling. I'd like to have at my disposal complicated
hybrid emotions, Germanic train-car constructions like, say, "the
happiness that attends disaster." Or: "the disappointment of
sleeping with one's fantasy." I'd like to show how "intimations of
mortality brought on by aging family members" connects with
"the hatred of mirrors that begins in middle age." I'd like to have a
word for "the sadness inspired by failing restaurants" as well as for
"the excitement of getting a room with a minibar."*
From: 'Middlesex' by Jeffrey Eugenides

It's true; sometimes there just doesn't seem to be one single
word that accurately describes how you're feeling about something or someone. Actually, though, there are often words to
describe specific experiences, emotions and feelings; they're
just not English words. That doesn't mean you can't use them
though!

Here's a few of those words: Start using them whenever they best describe your situation, your emotions and feelings.

Sisu – pronounced 'see-su' – is a Finnish word that describes stoic determination, focus, tenacity, bravery and resilience. If you hit a low and you're not sure if you can carry on, sisu is that bit extra you have in reserve, that somehow keeps you going. Ingrained in sisu is the understanding that life comes with difficulties and challenges. Sisu is about accepting these times and pressing on.

Kǔ qù gān lái – pronounced 'koo-jin-gan-lie'. After going through difficulties and tough times, in Chinese the word kǔ qù gān lái describes coming out the other side. It means 'from pain to sweetness'. It's the sense of happiness or relief you experience after going through adversity.

Hygge – pronounced hue-guh – is a Danish word for a mood of cosiness and comfortable conviviality with feelings of wellness and contentment. It derives from a sixteenth-century Norwegian term, hugga, meaning 'to comfort' or 'to console,' which is related to the English word 'hug'.

Dolce far niente – pronounced dolchay-far nee-entay – means 'sweet doing nothing'. It's the Italian concept of the enjoyment that comes from doing nothing without feeling guilty about it. When, for example, you sit outside a cafe with a coffee, watching the world go by. Time slows and you are aware of life in its simplicity, and you feel content. No stress, no pressure. All that matters is being in the moment; a 'doing nothing' moment.

MUSIC AND SONG

'How is it that music can, without words, evoke our laughter, our fears, our highest aspirations?' – Jane Swan

Music – both instrumental music and music with song – can help you access a range of feelings; from sadness to anger, happiness to joy. Music can move you to tears, soothe, calm and comfort you; it can uplift you, inspire and motivate you.

Music that you find beautiful and uplifting can provide hope and encouragement – Flaming Lips''Do you realise' for example, or Elbow's 'One day like this' or for something more upbeat – Mark Ronson's 'Uptown funk' or Fleetwood Mac's 'Don't stop thinking about tomorrow' and Primal Scream's 'Moving on up now'. These are just songs which came immediately to my mind; of course, you'll have your own favourites from one or many genres of music – classical, jazz, country or folk, reggae, R&B and so on.

Music has the ability to emphasise or change your mood completely. Listening to or playing music, singing and dancing to music can provide a focus that can range from being totally energising, to calming and relaxing. It can take you somewhere else and transport you back to happy or sad times and it can connect you to the future; give you the courage to do something and give you hope that things will turn out well.

Make a playlist of music and songs that uplift you. Sing out loud and dance like no one's watching. As with art, music and dancing can be different languages to express how you feel. Make your own music; if you don't already know how, learn to play an instrument; it's never too late!

Here's what others have said about music and song:

'Music gives a soul to the universe, wings to the mind, flight to the imagination, and life to everything.' – Plato

'Music was my refuge. I'd crawl into the space between the notes and curl my back to loneliness.' – Maya Angelou

'Music, once admitted to the soul, becomes a sort of spirit and never dies.' – Edward Bulwer-Lytton

'People haven't always been there for me. But music has.' – Taylor Swift

'When I hear music, I fear no danger. I am invulnerable. I see no foe. I am related to the earliest of times, and to the latest.' – Henry David Thoreau

'Music is the great uniter. An incredible force. Something that people who differ on everything and anything else can have in common.' – Sarah Dessen

'Music washes away from the soul the dust of everyday life.' – Berthold Auerbach

'Some days there won't be a song in your heart. Sing anyway.' – Emory Austin

'Where words leave off, music begins.' – Heinrich Heine

'My idea is that there is music in the air, music all around us; the world is full of it, and you simply take as much as you require.' – Edward Elgar

WARMING COMFORT

In her novel *The Bell Jar* Sylvia Plath wrote: 'There must be quite a few things a hot bath won't cure, but I don't know many of them. Whenever I'm sad I'm going to die, or so nervous I can't sleep, or in love with somebody I won't be seeing for a week, I slump down just so far and then I say: "I'll go take a hot bath."'

If you find taking a hot bath relaxing and it makes you feel good, recent research shows that there's good reason to take the plunge.

The findings of a study carried out at the University of Freiburg in Germany and reported in *New Scientist* in 2018 concluded that taking regular afternoon baths resulted in a moderate but persistent lift in mood for people taking part in the study.

Participants in the study who experienced moderate to severe depression were asked to sit in a 40°C (104°F) bath for 30 minutes twice a week for 8 weeks, then wrap themselves in a blanket and a hot water bottle for another 20 minutes.

How did a hot bath, warm blankets and a hot water bottle help lift the participants' mood? The researchers suggest it could be because the hot bath restores the body's natural temperature rhythm over the course of a day which, it's been found, can be disrupted in people who are depressed.

A list of things to warm you up:

A hot bath or shower
A hot water bottle
Blankets: fleece blankets, electric blankets, comfort blankets, weighted blankets
A heated mattress pad
Hand warmers
A foot warming mat
Microwaveable slippers
'Huffle-buffs'; the old, warm, comfortable clothes that you put on when you want to relax
Bed socks
Scarves and gloves
A fleece jumper
Clothes warmed on the radiator
A log fire
Hot drinks: tea, coffee, hot chocolate
Soups and stews

OVERCOMING LONELINESS

If you're lonely, you're not alone. Loneliness is something that most of us experience from time to time. You might experience loneliness as uncomfortable; a kind of sad emptiness. Or you might experience loneliness as a deprivation and pain which leaves you feeling isolated and desperate.

There are many different reasons why you might feel lonely: divorce, bereavement, physical or mental illness, disability, discrimination and unemployment, being a carer are common causes of loneliness. And although moving to a new area, new job or having a baby can be exciting and positive, people often find that new experiences can leave them feeling lonely.

If you feel lonely you *are* lonely. And it's not nice.

Human beings are social beings; we need to interact with others; to connect in positive ways and to feel that we are understood, that we belong and are valued by others. If you're lonely, there's nothing wrong with you; they might feel painful, but the lonely feelings are there to prompt you to connect with other people.

The problem is that feelings of loneliness can set off a downward spiral of negative thoughts and feelings which then leads to more intense feelings of loneliness which can serve to shut you down and close you off from others. However, the good news is that the downward spiral of negative thoughts also works in reverse; changing the way you think can lead to a change in feelings and behaviours which then generates an upward spiral out of loneliness.

Don't let the sadness and feelings of loneliness overwhelm you; make a decision to reach out and make some connections.

Do something. Relationships with other people don't have to be the only way to feel connected; hobbies and interests can also be an important source of stability and connection. If you have a hobby or interest that you can lose yourself in, you will find yourself actually searching out time to be by yourself in order to do what you enjoy. Creative pursuits: writing, painting, gardening, playing a musical instrument – and active pursuits such as yoga, swimming or running – can help you to feel engaged and connected.

Find like-minded people. Whatever you enjoy doing, do it with other people. Meetups, for example, www.meetup.com, enable you to meet local people who share your interests and enjoy doing the same things as you do. There's a wide range of interests and hobbies, plus some you've never thought of. The regular meetings will allow you to get to know others and build friendships.

Join or start a support group. If you are in a specific situation – you're a carer, have a chronic illness or disability – which leaves you feeling isolated and lonely, a support group can offer various forms of help, provide opportunities to share experiences and information. You can get a real sense of connection – feeling that you belong, and are with people who understand you.

Make a contribution. When you help other people, in the process, you help yourself. Volunteer for a cause. You'll meet other volunteers who also want to make a contribution to the lives of others – people with whom you can make a genuine connection. Search the internet for volunteering opportunities in your area. or go to ncvo.org.uk/ncvo-volunteering

Get a pet; a dog or a cat. Aside from companionship, pets can improve your psychological wellbeing.

SPENDING TIME WITH YOUR DOG

'Animals are such agreeable friends; they ask no questions; they pass no criticisms.' – George Eliot

It's true, animals can be a listening ear for whatever you want to talk about; they don't judge or criticise. Time spent with a cat or dog – simply stroking them – can be calming and comforting, providing an unconditional exchange of companionship, care and love.

Dogs not only sense when you are sad, they are simply great company; they are fun, give a sense of security and are another being to share the routine of the day with.

Your dog will be the first to greet you when you get home, even if you've only been out for ten minutes. Because dogs need to be walked, they get you out and moving in the fresh air. And, dogs love reggae. Really! A study by University of Glasgow and the Scottish SPCA, suggested that far from enjoying the strains of classical music, dogs are happier listening to soft rock or reggae. So if you like listening to Bob Marley and Black Uhuru or Fleetwood Mac and Jon Bon Jovi, it's likely that your dog will too.

If you'd love a dog but can't commit 24/7 go to www.borrowmydoggy.com. It connects dog owners with dog lovers in their neighbourhood to share the care of a dog. There are also opportunities for volunteers to interact with and care for animals at your local rspca.org.uk or animal sanctuary. And if you'd like to be a volunteer 'cat cuddler' Cats Protection, www.cats.org.uk/, say 'no matter how much time you can give, there's a place for you with us!'

STAY GROUNDED

FINDING SPIRITUALITY

'Just as a candle cannot burn without fire, we cannot live without a spiritual life.' – Buddha

Spirituality is a sense of being connected to and part of something that is bigger, more eternal than both yourself and the physical world.

For many people, a spiritual life is to be found from their religious beliefs: the connection to a higher being; the rituals, prayers, meditations or mantras involved. You don't have to be religious in order to be spiritual though. Even if you regard yourself as agnostic or an atheist, you can feel a sense of connection to something larger and more everlasting than yourself. You can choose to define what spirituality means for you in whatever way feels most appropriate. Concepts such as beauty, music and creativity, wildlife and the miracles of nature can all contribute to a sense of spirituality – to connecting to something profound, no matter how simple or awesome.

Spirituality can help you to feel grounded in the present and yet connected to the past and the future. People who are separated from their cultures, for example, may find that their shared spiritual beliefs and practices provide connections with their cultural identity.

Think about what you already do that makes you feel connected. Perhaps it's playing a team sport, singing in a choir, gardening or being outside with nature. Or it could be when you're at a sports match cheering your team along with thousands of other supporters. Maybe it's time spent singing and dancing with thousands of other music lovers at a music festival. Whatever it is – experience spirituality more often!

'The fact that I can plant a seed and it becomes a flower, share a bit of knowledge and it becomes another's, smile at someone and receive a smile in return, are to me, continual spiritual exercises.' – Leo Buscaglia

Find someone who is spiritual. Who do you already know who has balance and a sense of perspective; who has a calm concern and rapport with other people? It could be someone with a sense of wonder, someone who seeks out beauty and peace in the things they do. Spend time with spiritual people you admire. Their attitude will inspire you.

Get connected; support and become active in an organisation with a cause you believe in. Organisations such as Amnesty International, Save the Children or the World Wide Fund for Nature can connect you to other people and unite you in a common purpose. Or find a local charity that interests you; maybe one that promotes arts and culture or environmental concerns or works with children and young people? The positivity and sense of connection that can be gained from helping other people is a key aspect of spirituality.

FEELING GOOD ABOUT YOURSELF

Think of the last time you achieved something. Maybe you finished a difficult project or learned something new? Perhaps you passed a test or exam? Did you do something that required some courage on your part – perhaps you stood up to someone or walked away from a bad situation of some sort? Maybe you finally got round to completing some small task you'd been putting off for ages – Decorating a room, sorting out a pile of paperwork or cleaning out the fridge?

Of course, achievements come in all shapes and sizes but whatever it was, did you take the time to acknowledge your achievement or did you simply move on to the next thing without stopping to reflect; to acknowledge and congratulate yourself?

Be more aware of your achievements and give yourself some recognition. When you do something you're pleased about, stop for a minute and recognise it. Compliment yourself; tell yourself, 'Good for me! I've done OK.' Or, 'That went well, I'm pleased with myself.' Or 'That was bloody hard. But I did it.' Or 'All that effort paid off. Well done me!' or 'Hurrah! I'm brilliant!'

Think about times in the past where you've done well and felt good about yourself. Write them down. When you're not feeling good about yourself, and need something to uplift you, remind yourself of those occasions.

As well as recognising your abilities and achievements, do you accept the recognition that other people give you? If someone gives you a compliment, do you accept it and allow it to make you feel good? Or do you brush it off? Perhaps you don't want to appear immodest or the compliment or praise doesn't line up with how you see yourself. But when someone gives you a compliment it's the same as if they were giving you a gift. Therefore if you reject the compliment it's like rejecting – refusing to accept – a gift. That's not being nice to yourself or to the other person. Is it?!

Next time someone says something positive about you, accept what they're saying as a real possibility; that it is possible, for example, that you look great; that your hair looks nice today or that what you're wearing really suits you. Or that you've been thoughtful and considerate and it's made a positive difference to someone. Or that you've done something really well.

Believe the other person; they're being nice and they're being genuine. Aren't they? Be gracious; accept a compliment in the same way you would accept a gift; just say 'thank you'. And if you want to say more than that, simply 'How nice, thank you.' Or, 'Thank you. I really appreciate you telling me.'

And, you can make a note of the compliments that people pay you to read back when you're feeling low or doubting yourself.

BE INSPIRED BY OTHER PEOPLE

'Surround yourself only with people who are going to lift you higher.'
– Oprah Winfrey

Who do you know who has experienced major challenges and setbacks and yet, one way or another, managed to come through?

Perhaps you have a friend who has experienced injury or ill health or a family member whose life has been affected by alcoholism or drug addiction. Maybe you have a neighbour or colleague who has been through a relationship breakdown, domestic abuse or a bereavement. Perhaps it's someone you've read about who experienced a terrorist attack. It could be a celebrity, a sportsperson, a rock star or a politician who has overcome some form of adversity.

Although we all have to find our own way through difficulties and trauma, whoever it is and whatever they suffered, other people's experiences and stories of overcoming adversity can inspire you and reassure you that it is possible to come through crises.

When you're struggling with something in your life, other people's stories can awaken you to new possibilities. Their experiences can move you through apathy and despair to possibility and hope. Their stories can transform the way you perceive what you are capable of and give you a clear picture of what can be achieved.

As well as anyone you know who has coped with adversity, look for stories about people that inspire you: read and listen to stories about people who are inspiring. Take advantage of their knowledge and experience; get some insight into how to cope with difficulties and bounce back.

Malala Yousafzai and Matt Hampson are two young people who have inspired many others. Their bravery and determination could encourage you, too. Here are their stories.

In 2008, the Taliban banned girls from going to school in Malala Yousafzai's town in Swat Valley, Pakistan. Four years later, at the age of 15, after speaking out for girls' right to education, Malala was shot by a Taliban gunman. After months of surgeries, a move to the UK and rehabilitation Malala says: 'I knew I had a choice: I could live a quiet life or I could make the most of this new life I had been given. I determined to continue my fight until every girl could go to school. I established Malala Fund, a charity dedicated to giving every girl an opportunity to achieve a future she chooses.' In recognition of her work, Malala received the Nobel Peace Prize in December 2014 and became the youngest ever Nobel laureate: www.malala.org/

In a training session in 2005, a rugby scrum collapsed on top of Matt Hampson. At the age of 20, he was left paralysed from the neck down, breathing through a ventilator and needing 24-hour care. Matt has since decided to focus on the things he can still do and 'get busy living'. Matt's favourite film is *The Shawshank Redemption*, about a man condemned to a life in jail. Matt says 'There's a line in the film: "You get busy living or get busy dying." That's the grim reality you're left with when you find yourself paralysed in a wheelchair. I decided to get busy living, and to make the most of it in the process.' Matt established the Matt Hampson Foundation, www.matthampsonfoundation.org/, in 2011 to help others like him who have suffered similar catastrophic injuries through sport to receive the support they need to rebuild their lives.

HAVING PATIENCE

It's not easy to wake up day after day to discover you're still unwell or that your heart is still broken; that you haven't yet fully healed. But as you wait for things to get better, having patience can help.

Patience is the ability to wait calmly without needing to change a situation to when you think it should happen. With patience, there is understanding and trusting that things develop in their own time; that life is a process of unfolding. With patience, you know that there's a time for everything and everything takes time. This doesn't mean there isn't anything you can do to help the healing process along or for things to improve, but you will get there more easily if you have patience.

In a variety of situations, you may not even be aware that you're being impatient because your mind has already jumped ahead to how and where you want things to be.

Try to recognise when you're becoming impatient. Is your mind calm or agitated? Is your body relaxed or tensed? Stop fuelling your impatience with judgements about how unfair or how wrong it all is. Tell yourself 'This too will pass'. Time always passes, and how you feel during that time is of your own making.

Having patience may not make the process go more quickly, but it can make it more manageable. Shift your thoughts about the time something is taking to happen and you'll arrive with a calmer, clearer mind and attitude.

one day,

at

a time

GAINING PERSPECTIVE

'Perspective is everything when you are experiencing the challenges of life.' – Joni Earecksom Tada

When problems and difficulties happen, when major life changes come along, things can often feel overwhelming, unmanageable and never ending.

Gaining perspective can help. Gaining perspective means being able to see the relationship between what's happening within your world and what's happening outside it. It means getting a sense of where you are in the greater scheme of things; taking everything else into account. It means recognising and understanding the relative importance of things.

Perspective involves being rational. The word 'rational' is derived from the word 'ratio' which suggests that being rational is to see things in proportion and in perspective.

If, for example, you were upset about an argument with a friend or you were disappointed that you didn't get the job, being rational and getting things into perspective can help you recognise that, as difficult to manage as it is right now, the situation will change; life will continue and things will work out.

Ask someone over the age of 70 about their life. What went well and what didn't? You'll learn that they also had feelings of fear, sadness and struggle, just like you have right now. How did things turn out for them? How do they now view some of those problems when seen in relation to everything else that happened in their life? Be aware that right now you are the one living the life you will speak of when you are older.

Situations that turn life upside DOWN can often shift PERSPECTIVE to right-side UP

TO EVERYTHING, A SEASON

To every thing there is a season, and a time to every purpose under the heaven;

A time to be born, and a time to die; a time to plant, and a time to reap that which is planted;

A time to kill, and a time to heal; a time to break down, and a time to build up;

A time to weep, and a time to laugh; a time to mourn, and a time to dance;

A time to cast away stones, and a time to gather stones together; a time to embrace, and a time to refrain from embracing;

A time to get, and a time to lose; a time to keep, and a time to cast away;

A time to rend, and a time to sew; a time to keep silence, and a time to speak;

A time to love, and a time to hate; a time of war, and a time of peace.

Ecclesiastes 3: 1–8

THE CHINESE FARMER'S TALE

This is believed to be a Taoist parable about going with the flow in life. Just like a river, life takes you on a journey regardless whether it's good or bad.

On a certain day, one of the farmer's horses escaped. That evening, all the neighbours came around and said to him 'That's too bad!' And he said, 'Maybe.'

The next day the horse came back, and brought seven wild horses with it. And all the neighbours came around and said, 'Well that's great. Isn't it?' And he said, 'Maybe.'

The next day, as his son was attempting to tame one of his horses and was riding it, he fell down and broke his leg. The neighbours came again in the evening and said, 'Well that's too bad. Isn't it?' And he said, 'Maybe.'

The next day the conscription officers came around to recruit people into the army but they rejected his son because he had a broken leg. All the people came around and said, 'That's great.' And he said, 'Maybe.'

The moral of the story as the philosopher Alan Watts tells it is that 'the whole process of nature is a process of immense complexity and it is really impossible to tell whether something that happens in it is good or bad. Because you never know the consequences of the misfortune. Or, you never know the consequences of good fortune.'

READING POSITIVE NEWS

Minimise the amount of negative news in your life. You're rarely better informed, your life isn't better off and you rarely feel better about yourself, other people or the world around you for having read low-level, negative information.

Most of us have a number of sources of information that we could eliminate from our day with no detriment to our lives whatsoever. While staying up to date can keep you informed and enable you to take part in discussions, it can also mean your life is filled with irrelevant or unnecessary information. News and information overload is to the mind what sugar is to the body: empty calories that give you a rush but then bring you down and leave you feeling like crap. You wouldn't want to stuff your body with low-quality food. Why fill your mind with low-quality thoughts?

There is a wide range of events – the economy, war and terrorism, the behaviour of celebrities and political scandal – over which you have little or no control but you can easily consume more and more information about them. This drains your time and energy and can leave you feeling stressed, helpless and negative simply because you have little or no control.

Read more positive news. There's more to the world than bad news. Away from the conflict, disaster and misanthropy, there is good news: solutions and improvements, ideas and inventions, altruism and kindness, supportive movements and organisations.

Look for uplifting stories that celebrate the best of life and be inspired by the good in the world around us. Watch and read motivational stories or speeches. TED talks, for example, are inspiring, educational and motivating, see www.ted.com

Online, you can find websites dedicated to sharing inspiring and positive news from around the world.

http://positivenews.org.uk/

http://www.goodnewsnetwork.org/

https://www.theguardian.com/world/series/the-upside

http://www.dailygood.org/

When you come across something that resonates and uplifts you, let others know about it on social media; share it with your friends.

MANAGING STRESS

'For fast-acting relief, try slowing down.' – Lily Tomlin

What's a busy day at work, study or at home like for you? What are you doing? What are you thinking? What do you have to do next? What haven't you done? How do you feel?

At one time or another most of us experience busy periods at work, with study or home life; there's much to do and much to think about. You're doing several things at once and time just races by.

You're caught up with what you haven't done and what you've yet to do and your mind is chattering away with judgements and commentary.

Different people find different events and situations more or less stressful than others. We each have things – deadlines, delays, doing several things at once, feeling overwhelmed by what you haven't done and what you've yet to do, other people's needs and demands – that are particularly stressful for us.

Most of us might be able to cope with one thing we find stressful but when difficult situations and challenges mount up it can become a real struggle to cope. Feelings of stress overtake your mind and prevent you from thinking clearly. What to do?

You need to calm down the emotional part of your brain and engage the rational reasoning part of your brain so that you can work out what practical things you can do to manage and reduce the stress.

Get some breathing space. You can do this anywhere at any time. Simply take a couple of minutes to stop what you're doing and focus on breathing. Breathe in. As you you breathe out, at some point, stop for one second. Then continue exhaling – as much as you can. Do this for a minute or two. Getting some breathing space will help calm you down, collect and clarify your thoughts. During busy, stressful periods, try to get some breathing space two or three times a day.

Once you can think straight, prioritise; work out what's important, what really needs to be done. Plan what you need to do. Think through the steps you need to take and how you will do them. It's easier to get straight on to the next step if you have already planned what and how you are going to do it. It allows you to maintain a steady pace and keep the pace going. Tell yourself 'I have a plan. I can manage this.'

Slow down. Do everything 20% slower. It might feel weird, but physically slowing down not only gives your brain the opportunity to think and come up with ways to manage the stress, but also, the mere act of slowing down makes you less stressed. Try it!

Give yourself more time. Reduce your commitments and give each commitment more time. Don't plan things close together; instead, leave room between activities and tasks. If you're constantly rushing from one thing to another, give things more time. If you think it only takes you 30 minutes to get some-where, perhaps give yourself 45 minutes so you can go at a leisurely pace and not get stressed if delays occur on the way.

COMFORTING FOOD

Of course you need to eat a healthy balanced diet. But if you've had a difficult day – failed a test, lost or broken something, clashed with a colleague, been let down by a friend or family member, or you're unwell or in pain, you need to indulge in comfort food – soups and stews, pizzas and pasta dishes, curries or a risotto, a plate of mashed potato or a big mug of hot chocolate – whatever you love.

Nourishing ingredients and hearty portions are an easy and delicious way to soothe the soul. Comfort food gives both comfort and joy; whether you're slurping a bowl of steaming hot chicken pho or chomping your way through a pile of hot buttered toast, comfort food is ... well, it's comforting! Comfort food consoles, reassures and gives cheer.

Comfort food can connect us to family traditions, happy memories and cherished moments and loved ones. Comfort food is often a favourite from childhood; something your Mum or Dad made you when you were unwell or upset, in an effort to help you feel better.

The writer Maya Angelou has said that for her, 'the best comfort food will always be greens, cornbread, and fried chicken'.

What are your favourite comfort foods?

FIVE SENSES MEDITATION

Whenever things feel off balance and out of your control, the five senses meditation can connect and engage you directly and immediately with the present moment, allowing you to feel grounded, no matter what's going on around you.

1. Look – really look – around you and notice that you can see. Search for something that you don't normally notice, like something tiny or something up high. Notice colours, shapes, symmetry and patterns.

2. Be aware of something that you can feel. Notice the texture – the rough or the smooth, the hardness or the softness, the warmth or the coldness – of something.
Feel your feet in your shoes.
Rub lotion on your hands.
Put your hands under running water.
Snap a rubber band on your wrist.
Take a hot or cool shower.
Take a piece of clothing, a blanket or a towel and knead it in your hands or hold it against your face.
Pop some bubble wrap.

3. Breathe in a smell.
Scented flowers – roses, jasmine, lavender and honey-suckle
Herbs and spices
A scented candle
The smoke from an extinguished match.

4. Taste something.
Bite into a lemon or lime.
Suck on a mint sweet.
Eat some corn flakes, crackers or crisps; something that also has a distinct texture and makes a lot of noise.

5. Listen.
Listen to music.
Read something out loud: a poem, a song or something from a book.
Listen to someone else talk – on the radio or an audio-book or podcast.

INDULGING IN SMALL PLEASURES

There's a wealth of small pleasures which can bring you moments of comfort and joy every day. We all have things that we enjoy, that give us pleasure and moments of happiness. Life is a collection of moments and the more happy moments we have, the more often we are happy!

What, for you, makes for small pleasures? Maybe eating the froth on the cappuccino is a small pleasure. Maybe it's eating a perfectly ripe peach or pear. Perhaps you get pleasure from the flowers that you've picked from your garden. Or you enjoy foraging for wild blackberries in the autumn. As odd as it may seem to other people maybe one of your small pleasures is time spent ironing pillowcases?

What about a lie in? An afternoon nap? Or a foot massage? A bubble bath or a hot shower? Perhaps it's sitting in front of an open fire or sitting in the sun or a walk in the rain. Is car dancing one of your favourite things? Spotting dogs who look like their owners?

When you make an effort to take notice of what's happening around you that pleases you, you'll be surprised at just how many things give moments of pleasure. On the next two pages you can make a list of small pleasures and favourite things, the ordinary and the extraordinary, the familiar and the new, the small things and the tiny things, the cheap and the expensive and do them more often. Add to your list every time you think of something else that brings a small pleasure.

it's often the little things that hold the greatest meaning

MY SMALL PLEASURES

....
....
....
....
....
....
....
....
....
....
....
....
....
....
....
....

81

GETTING TO SLEEP

If you're having trouble sleeping it could be that worry, anxiety or stress is keeping you awake. Thoughts and worries seem to grow and loom larger at night; you need to switch off and sleep but your brain keeps talking to itself; your mind is in overdrive thinking about what you did or didn't do, what has or hasn't happened or what you have yet to face or do. Even if you could do something, night time is not usually a practical time to do anything about whatever it is that's keeping you awake.

Perhaps, though, your mind isn't racing, you're not caught up in troubling thoughts. You just can't get to sleep! But whatever the reason for your sleeplessness, although you can't make yourself go to sleep, there are things you can do that may help.

Before you get into bed, create for yourself a calm, relaxing bed-time routine. Decide what things are most relaxing to you and you enjoy doing at the end of the day; it may include walking the dog, having a shower or bath, reading, and/or listening to music or a podcast. Your routine could take 10–20 minutes, or it could take up to an hour. Whatever works for you.

Once you're in bed, if you don't soon fall asleep, do not berate yourself. When you lie there telling yourself 'I'm still awake. I'm never going to get to sleep. It's not fair. I'm going to feel horrible tomorrow. It's not fair! ' you're just creating a stress response that makes the problem worse.

Write it down. If you can't fall asleep because of concerns about, for example, money and work, relationships, family or health worries, you may find it useful to write them down. This helps because you're externalising your thoughts; getting them out of your head and down onto paper.

Try Jacobson's Relaxation Technique – also known as progressive relaxation therapy. You consciously tense and relax your muscles, one after the other, starting with your toes and working up your body, releasing tension as you go. Put 'Jacobson's Relaxation Technique' into a search engine to find out how to do it.

Don't keep looking at the clock. Turn the clock around so you can't see it. Fixating on the changing time is definitely not going to help you relax and fall asleep.

Think positive thoughts. Reflecting on the positives in your day can shift your attention away from troubling thoughts and help you to feel more calm. Simply think of three good things that happened for you during the day. See pages 8 and 9. Remembering the good things – no matter how small – that happened during the day helps stop your mind from going round in circles.

Listen to something. Listening to something on the radio, listening to music, an audiobook or a podcast can distract your mind, giving it something else to engage with.

Open your eyes. If you're lying in bed and are unable to sleep, try keeping your eyes open. As they start to close, tell yourself to resist. Often the more you try to stay awake, the sleepier you become.

REMINISCING AND NOSTALGISING

Whether it's triggered by a song, a photo, a diary or a treasured possession, nostalgia evokes a particular time or experience, person or place. Nostalgic thoughts are often triggered by our senses – sights, sounds, smells and/or tastes – that take us back to particular times, events, people and places; schooldays, for example, a place you once lived or worked, friends or family members, holidays, festivals and sports events.

We tend to become nostalgic when we feel sad and especially if we feel lonely and disconnected from others. Although nostalgia might be triggered by difficulties and feelings of loneliness, like Odysseus – the hero of Homer's epic poem the Odyssey, who used memories of his family and home to get through his difficulties and struggles – you may find that reminiscing – looking back on happy times, experiences, people and events – and nostalgia – the feelings of both warmth and sadness that come as a result of reminiscing – can provide comfort and moments of joy.

Do draw on happy memories when you need a lift, but be careful to enjoy them without idealising the past. It's easy to look back and believe that everything was so much better then – that you were happier. But idealising the past often means forgetting, minimising or ignoring the difficulties that may also have occurred during those times. As Mick Jagger once said 'The past is a great place, but I don't want to be its prisoner.'

A simple, easy wasy to reminisce is to flip though old photos or photo albums. What good memories come to mind? What were the circumstances? Who else is in the photos?

Think of a song or piece of music that you associate with some good times in the past. What were the circumstances and who is the person or the people you associate with this memory?

What smells or scents, foods or tastes take you back to a happy time or event?

Get together with a friend or family member and share some good memories. Reminiscing with someone else can help renew your connections as you remember your shared history.

Time spent reminiscing and nostalgising is an enjoyable way to feel connected to people, experiences and events in the past. But reminiscing doesn't just have to be about your past it can also be about your future.

Although there is the sadness that certain people, places and events are in the past, those memories can give you hope for the future, knowing that the good times and feelings – the happiness or fulfillment – you experienced then can be found again in different circumstances, with other people, in other places.

So let the past inspire your future: create new memories. What you do now will become the memories you cherish and hold dear in future. Whatever does or doesn't happen next – you'll always have happy memories to draw on. As Humphrey Bogart told Ingrid Bergman at the end of the film *Casablanca*: 'We'll always have Paris.'

LAUGHING MORE

'He who laughs, lasts.' – Mary Pettibone Poole

It feels good to laugh. Something strikes you as funny and right there and then the laughter and the joy of being in the moment are all you are about. So why not make a resolution to laugh more? Aiming to laugh more is just as important as aiming to get more exercise, eat more healthily and drink more water.

Here are some ideas to help you:

Do more of what you know makes you laugh. When was the last time you had a really good laugh? What were you doing? Do more of that.

Start the day with an episode of one of your favourite sit-coms. Or an amusing radio or podcast series. Or watch YouTube clips of one of your favourite comedians or other funny clips; watch Man gobbles at turkeys turkeys gobble back. Follow funny people via their posts on Twitter.

Make friends with a funny person. Some people are naturally funny. They might have a way with words, or a wacky way of looking at the world. Maybe you just find the same things funny; you have a shared sense of humour. As the actress Audrey Hepburn once said: 'I love people who make me laugh. I honestly think it's the thing I like most, to laugh. It cures a multitude of ills. It's probably the most important thing in a person.' So, if you find someone who makes you laugh, befriend them. Or marry them.

even
a small bit
of :joy: has the
power
to lift Big
things

FINDING FLOW

Think about the times – even short periods of time – when you're so absorbed in what you were doing that time passed without you realising. What's happening? What are you doing during those periods?

Perhaps you were reading, listening to music, the radio, a podcast or audiobook or watching TV. Perhaps it was a musical instrument or a video game you were playing. Maybe you were cooking, gardening or it was an arts and crafts activity. Whatever it was, as you did it, no other thoughts entered your mind because you were completely focused and engaged in what you were doing; you didn't even notice the time that was passing.

When you're doing something that keeps you effortlessly focused and engaged like this, you're experiencing something known as 'flow'. When you're in a state of flow, it's as though a water current is effortlessly carrying you along. Your awareness merges with what you're doing and you are completely 'in the moment'. Your thoughts are positive and in tune with what you're doing.

What do you like doing? What activities can you engage with for half an hour – a crossword, a jigsaw or sudoku – or immerse yourself in for an hour or more? Swimming? Running? Fishing? Birdwatching? Maybe you enjoy cooking?

Identify the things you enjoy doing. Know that they are activities where you can easily experience flow and that can be an important source of familiarity and comfort and provide stability and contentment.

Plan ahead. Make a list of activities and interests that you can 'lose yourself' in, whether it's for half an hour, a few hours or a weekend. Doing things that you enjoy can help you move through low points. As well as hobbies, sports and interests you might already like doing, here are a few more ideas:

Books and films. It could be a thriller, science fiction or comedy. Whatever the genre, as events unfold, you become lost in the story. At your local library, you can borrow books for free. DVDs, CDs, audiobooks are available to borrow for a small fee. Charity shops are also good for books, audiobooks, DVDs and CDs.

Get creative. Whether it's doodling, drawing or painting, embroidery, sculpture, cake decorating, calligraphy, origami or one of dozens of different art and craft activities, doing something creative can be a positive way of being focused and engaged.

Often, you need little in the way of materials. With drawing, for example, all you need is some paper and a pencil. Think you can't draw? Yes, you can. Writing in the *Sunday Times* in 2021, journalist India Knight suggested: 'Buy a copy of *Drawing on the Right Side of the Brain* by Betty Edwards (in print since 1979 for good reason) and read it properly – no skipping straight to the exercises – before sitting down with paper and pencil and following instructions. You will quickly amaze and delight yourself. Hands down the best and most life-enhancing thing I've done in lockdown.'

MANAGING DISAPPOINTMENT

'There's a bit of magic in everything, and some loss to even things out.' – Lou Reed

Being turned down for a place on a course, a job, a flat or a house, are all sources of disappointment. So are seeing your team lose, bad weather upsetting your plans, failing an exam, someone withdrawing their support, or a meeting at work or a social occasion not going as well as you'd hoped.

Disappointment happens when things don't go the way you expected that they would. Even when you try to forget about it, a disappointment can stay hovering in the back of your mind like a grey cloud. This is a perfectly natural response to the hurt and sadness that occurs when your expectations or hopes fail to materialise.

Whenever a situation leaves you feeling disappointed, you need to sit with it; to take time to acknowledge and accept that what has happened has happened and nothing can change that. You then need to see what there is to learn from your disappointment and move on.

Of course, it's not always easy to move on. But continually dwelling on what failed to materialise, what did or didn't happen – the 'didn't really hit it off' date, for example, or the sale that didn't go through – can keep you stuck and make it difficult to think and act constructively on your situation. It won't happen automatically, you have to decide that you are going to move on.

Acknowledge your disappointment. Although you should avoid wallowing in your disappointment, don't suppress or deny it either. Be honest with yourself – in your head or out loud, say how you feel. Once you've acknowledged the disappointment, you are in a better position to look forward.

Think like a sports fan. Sports fans and sports participants know that whenever they or their team lose, staying stuck in disappointment is not helpful. They let go of negative thinking and instead move on to think about the next game or race and the opportunities it will present. So, to leave disappointment behind, do the same; make a decision that you are going to move on.

Focus on thinking about what can be done rather than what wasn't or can't be done. Be open to new ideas and new ways of doing things. Rather than thinking, 'I should/shouldn't have ...' Try saying 'It might help to ...' or 'I could ...' or 'now I'm going to ...'

Think back to the last time that you were disappointed. What did you learn? Did you even stop to reflect on this? By reflecting on what happened and what went wrong, you can identify what you've learnt that will help you avoid similar disappointments and setbacks in the future.

Anticipate future disappointment. Having a back-up plan will not only help you feel secure but will also lessen the disappointment if things don't work out. Supposing, for example, you don't get the job. If you have already applied for other jobs, but you don't get this one, you've got other job possibilities to think about. As the writer Alain de Botton says: 'One of the best protections against disappointment is to have a lot going on.'

ACCEPTING THAT ALL THINGS COME AND GO

Everything that comes into this world also leaves it. Just as the seasons come and go, so do night and day, sun and rain, the ocean waves, health and wealth, war and peace. Nothing is permanent and all eventually ends.

Mindfulness can help you to understand this; to appreciate the happy times and to make the most of now, knowing it will pass. The chocolate meditation is a way to remind yourself of the passing of pleasure. Simply place a piece of chocolate or a toffee into your mouth. Be aware of, appreciate and enjoy it as it slowly melts away.

Just as pleasure doesn't last, neither do difficulties and problems. One way or another, they will pass too. Think back to a difficult time; a time when you had a setback, a challenge or a problem to deal with. However long it lasted, it wasn't permanent. One way or another it passed. Things may not have worked out the way you wanted them to, but they didn't remain the same. The ice cube meditation is a reminder that problems and difficulties pass too. Place an ice cube on the palm of your hand. As it slowly melts, it will probably be uncomfortable, painful even. But the ice cube does melt and the discomfort does end.

When you're experiencing adversity, reminding yourself that the difficulties will lessen and eventually pass can give you hope: an ability to look to the future and trust that things will turn out OK.

Vita Summa Brevis Spem Nos Vetat Incohare Longam

They are not long, the weeping and the laughter,

    Love and desire and hate:

I think they have no portion in us after

    We pass the gate.

They are not long, the days of wine and roses:

    Out of a misty dream

Our path emerges for a while, then closes

    Within a dream.

Ernest Dowson's poem describes how all things pass. Weeping and laughter, love, desire and hate, he wrote, do not last long. And neither, he said, do the days of pleasure and happiness – which he beautifully described as 'the days of wine and roses'. And as for your life, it is like a path seen coming out of a mist, then disappearing into that same mist.

BEGINNING AGAIN

'Every new beginning comes from some other beginning's end.' – Seneca

It's true. Everything has a beginning and everything has an end. Endings bring change. And change means that things will be different.

Whether it's the end of a relationship or friendship, good friends or close family moving away, the end of a job or finishing university, the prospect of change can leave you feeling vulnerable, facing an uncertain future, not knowing what to expect and often assuming the worst. You may worry if you'll be able to adjust to the change in circumstances and if things will work out well.

You might not be able to control a particular change in your life or stop it from happening, but you can control how you respond to change. A beginner's mind can help.

Beginner's mind is a concept from mindfulness. Beginner's mind encourages you to start afresh, with no preconceived ideas about how things will be. Beginner's mind doesn't ignore or dismiss how things were before, but rather than cling to situations from the past, beginner's mind encourages you to take a new perspective and to respond to things as they now are.

Practise making changes and see that you can cope with change and begin again. Drive, walk or cycle a different route to somewhere you regularly go. Take a different route from your normal one around the supermarket. Move the clock or the kitchen bin to a different place in the room. Yes, the change will seem disconcerting at first, but you will get used to it.

amid
the
darkness
OF AN
ENDING

Please Leave A Light ON For A New Beginning

BUILDING YOUR COURAGE

The word 'courage' comes from the French word 'coeur', which means 'heart'. Courage is a state of the heart. It's also the state of mind or spirit that enables you to face difficulty despite your concerns. It's the ability to do what feels right, even though it scares you. Courage is what makes you brave and helps you take action.

Each day there may be situations where you need to make a courageous choice. Maybe you need the courage to ask for advice and help. You might need courage to admit to a mistake or to walk away from someone or something, to stand up for yourself or to make a decision that others won't like.

Courage comes from being motivated by a clear goal. Focusing on why you're doing something can help stop feelings of doubt, uncertainty and fear from paralysing you. Of course, situations that require courage often mean taking a risk that something could go wrong. Don't let that stop you! Instead, acknowledge your doubts and then decide what you will do if things don't work out; what your plan B will be.

There's two ways you can build your courage. Firstly, do one small thing every day that scares you and feel your courage grow. Doing one small thing every so often will help maintain the strength you need to be courageous for the big things. Secondly, think of a situation in the past when, even though you felt afraid, you took action. Who or what helped you? What thoughts or feelings encouraged you? Remind yourself of that, next time you need courage.

big BRAVE moments are often paved
with small BRAVE choices

SAYING AFFIRMATIONS

Affirmations – positive statements about yourself and your abilities – can help support you and encourage you. They can strengthen your courage and your confidence; your beliefs in your abilities.

Affirmations don't deny or ignore difficulties; often, an affirmation includes an acknowledgement of the difficulty. For example, ' I may be sad/anxious/angry/but I can still deal with this', but the focus and emphasis is on the positive.

It's important to find affirmations that resonate with you. Some that you may have come across may be a bit too woo-woo, for example: 'The universe provides for me in abundance.' Or they're simply not true: 'You only fail if you quit.' (What's more true is that you only fail if you don't know when to quit!)

Affirmations such as 'I get by with a little help from my friends' and 'I've managed before, I can do so again' are more believable because you've got by with a little help from your friends in the past or you have managed before.

You can say affirmations out loud in front of a mirror. Or simply say them in your head. You may want to ask a friend or family member to support you with affirmations. Listening to someone else repeat your affirmations can help reinforce your belief in them. In fact, when it comes to persuading yourself about something, research shows that, in a variety of situations, if you address yourself by your own name, your chances of doing well can increase significantly. It might seem weird, but it can focus your thinking and motivate you. Rather than telling yourself, for example, 'I can do this', address yourself using your name, 'Amy, you can do this.'

Below are some affirmations; positive statements that offer reassurance that you can make it through a difficult situation. Choose a couple of affirmations from the list that are meaningful and believable for you. Then, on the next two pages, write them out and add to them some of your own. Then, when you need courage and confidence, repeat one or more until you start to feel calmer or stronger.

One step at a time

I can do this

I'm going to focus on my breathing until I know what to do

I'm going to face this situation the best that I can

I've managed before and I can do so again

I'm stronger than I think

One way or another, things will work out

It's OK to feel this way, it's a normal reaction

This may be difficult, but it will pass

I can get through this

MY AFFIRMATIONS

....
....
....
....
....
....
....
....
....
....
....
....
....
....
....

BEING IN AWE

Awe. It's a combination of feelings – wonder, reverence, admiration and fear – as a result of experiencing something beautiful, sublime, grand or powerful.

'Awe is a positive emotion triggered by awareness of something vastly larger than the self and not immediately understandable, such as nature, art, music, or being caught up in a collective act such as a ceremony, concert or political march,' says Dacher Keltner, professor of psychology at the University of California, Berkeley. In 2020, Professor Keltner and his colleagues carried out a study which showed that regularly experiencing awe is a simple way to boost our emotional wellbeing.

In the study, participants took 15-minute 'awe walks' once a week for eight weeks. They were asked to tap into their sense of curiosity and child-like wonder; to consciously be aware of and appreciate the world around them. As a result, participants reported increased positive emotions and less distress in their daily lives.

One of the key features of awe is that it promotes a positive sense of perspective between yourself and the bigger picture and power of the world around you. There's a sense of feeling small in the grand scheme of things. But isn't feeling small a negative thing? Yes, but with awe experiences, it's your problems that shrink rather than your sense of self-worth.

Awe is something that Jake Tyler regularly experienced between 2016 and 2018. At 30 years old he was overweight, had a drinking problem and with many years of feeling broken, Jake was suicidal. He was signed off work and spent most days walking the family dog, Reggie. Jake says that his walks helped him understand that 'The world is pretty amazing and nature is lovely'. Realising how healing being outside had been for him, Jake was inspired to do an epic 3000-mile walk circumnavigating Britain. It took some planning, the walk wasn't easy, but Jake says: 'Everything felt completely stripped back. I was on my own in this natural setting and I felt reset. I realised everything had been here before and would be here long after me. I felt insignificant but in a good way, a way that made me wonder at it all rather than making me feel small.' You can read more about Jake's journey in his book *A Walk from the Wild Edge*.

Of course, oceans and landscapes, sunsets and starry skies can all prompt feelings of awe but so can the delicacy and intricacy of a spider's web or noticing flowers growing through a crack in the pavement. The built environment and the technological marvels that surround you can also prompt awe.

Experience more awe in your life; seek out the things that create awe for you. If you have a limited ability to get out and about, looking at the changing sky outside your window or watching nature programmes such as the BBC's 'Planet Earth' can give you a sense of wonder and appreciation for the world you live in.

THE POWER OF POETRY

Poems streamline thoughts, emotions and experience to short, direct sentences. With the minimum of words, poetry can describe what we already know or feel but haven't been able to express as eloquently as the poet.

Poems play with language; there is significance in each and every word and where each word is placed. As the writer Michael Morpurgo has observed: 'A poet is a distiller. He or she distils feelings, insights, impressions, notions and the best poets do this in such a way that we never want to forget what they have written.'

Poems define the smallest moments of our lives. Poems can change the way we think about things, they can draw our attention to things that we often pass by or take for granted.

Poems can help us understand ourselves, our feelings and our relationship with the world. The words and sentiments in a poem can let us know that we are not alone, that our fears, doubts and sorrows have been felt by others before. As the poet Dylan Thomas wrote: 'Poetry is what in a poem makes you laugh, cry, prickle, be silent, makes your toenails twinkle, makes you want to do this or that or nothing, makes you know that you are alone in the unknown world, that your bliss and suffering is forever shared and forever all your own.'

Start collecting poems that comfort and uplift you. Below are some ideas to get you started. Google them to read them in full. You can watch *Still I Rise* being read by Maya Angelou on YouTube.

Still I Rise. By Maya Angelou

They are not long. By Ernest Dowson

People need people. By Benjamin Zephaniah

Leisure. By William Henry Davies

'Hope' is the thing with feathers. By Emily Dickinson

One of the best things about learning poetry is that if you've learnt it off by heart, the poem becomes part of you, to carry with you wherever you go. Learning poetry is not as difficult as you might think; you just need to learn a couple of lines at a time. First, read the poem out loud to yourself a few times. Then, take two lines at a time; learn just two per day. Write out the poem on the next two days. Whenever possible, say the lines of the poem out loud, so that you're listening to the words as well as saying them. Hearing the poem with your ears will help you pick up on rhymes and rhythms that will help you memorise the poem. Practise often: walking to work, walking the dog, cleaning and cooking, in the shower, on a run.

'I find learning a poem especially helpful when I'm awake in the small hours. There's something hugely comforting in the mind's secure possession of a literary work.' – Rachel Kelly, writer and mental health campaigner.

A POEM TO REMEMBER

....

....

....

....

....

....

....

....

....

....

....

....

....

....

....

CREATING HOPE AND MOVING ON

'If somebody hurts you, it's okay to cry a river. Just remember to build a bridge and get over it.' – Taylor Swift

What if it feels like you'll never get better, or you can't get over something that's happened to you, that nothing is going to change, that you won't be able to move on? The thing is, things do change and you can move on. But not until you decide that you want to move forward and you are going to move on.

Hope encourages you to believe that things will eventually improve and be good and that you'll feel better.

Hope is not a switch you can simply turn on, but hope is something you can create. How? Well, rather than dwell on what's passed and what's out of your control – which makes you feel hopeless – you start thinking about what you *can* control. And that helps you to feel hopeful. You take small steps to build your hope up every day by working on the things you do have some control over and can achieve.

You can create hope by setting one or two goals for yourself.

There's always something you can do in the present to work towards something you'd like to do in the future. Aim to achieve one step towards a larger goal each day or every few days. Doing this will help you feel that, step by step, things can change for the better and that you do have some control.

EASING BACK INTO LIFE AFTER AN ILLNESS

As you start to feel better, it can be tempting to throw yourself back into your usual routine. But pushing yourself to take two steps forward could mean you then find yourself going three steps back. If you've been physically unwell or injured, even if you feel better, your body will be weak from the illness and your immune system needs to regain its strength. Know that energy you use up doing everyday things is energy diverted from getting better. Be kind to your body. Have patience, take it slowly, one step at a time.

Illness makes us slow down, so when you're getting back on your feet, you need to do simple things. Things that don't take up too much time and energy. Write a letter or email to someone you haven't caught up with in a while, go through old photos, declutter a cupboard or a shelf or just clear your coat pockets or bag of receipts, train tickets etc. Small, simple tasks can seem like a chore when you're in the midst of a busy life, but when you're unwell those little tasks might provide the simplicity and just the right pace for you and won't take much energy either.

You might like to keep an 'achievement journal.' Note the things, no matter how small, you achieved that day. (A 'Ta – da! list' rather than a 'To do list.') When you're going through a difficult time in your life and are struggling to feel better, noting small achievements will help you to see that you can do things and you can build on those things to help you move on.

What gets included may depend on how you're feeling that day. Sometimes it might simply be that you got out of bed and got dressed. Sometimes it might be household chores or work tasks that you completed. There's a wide variety of things in our lives that make for small achievements. Maybe, for example, you sent an email to enquire about something or had a chat on the phone with a friend or read a couple of chapters in a book, made a new recipe, listened to the news or cleaned the bathroom. Maybe today was the day you went out with friends for the first time in ages or you booked a holiday. Perhaps you returned to work.

Regularly write in an achievement journal and every now and then you'll be able to look back through your journal to reflect on all that you've learned and achieved. It will all add up to quite a lot of small achievements!

MANAGING SETBACKS

Even when you think you're doing well – you're recovering, bouncing back from adversity – you can expect that, every now and again, you'll have bad days. Weeks, months, a year or more after a difficult time in your life, you might have days when, although it felt like there was no reason at all to feel knocked back, you just did. If you're having a bad day, especially if it's after a period of better days, there's no need to wonder 'what's wrong with me?' Bad days do happen. They will pass. Accept that sometimes you may have a bad day for an obvious reason or for no apparent reason. On those days, be kind and gentle with yourself. Phone a friend, stay in and eat pizza and have an early night. Or whatever works for you.

As the Austrian poet Rainer Maria Rilke said: 'Let everything happen to you: beauty and terror. Just keep going. No feeling is final.'

If, however, you're concerned that you're not able to move forward, ask for help. You might want to talk through the things you're finding challenging with a trained professional. Talking therapies can help with many difficult life problems – from coping with traumatic experiences and events, to dealing with depression and anxiety or managing harmful behaviours.

Ask your GP for advice about seeing a therapist or counsellor or find an accredited therapist at the British Association of Counsellors and psychotherapists (BACP): www.bacp.co.uk.

CREATING A COMFORT BOX

When you're having a hard time it can be a real effort to do anything at all, let alone find something that will comfort you or lift your mood. You may then find it helpful to have already created a comfort box.

The idea of a comfort box is that it contains things that you find comforting; things that ground you and help you feel calm. Things to focus your mind on, to distract you and to help you feel better. With a comfort box, you have what you need to hand; the things that you find helpful are easily accessible. Of course, this will be different for everyone, but here are some ideas for what you might add to your comfort box:

- Something to distract you: a sketchbook or colouring book, a puzzle book, sudoku, word search or a book of crosswords.
- A few photos of friends and family members and/or pets you love.
- A few photos of places that have positive memories attached to them.
- Your list of small pleasures.
- YouTube clips of uplifting videos.
- Cards or a notebook in which you've written some positive affirmations, uplifting quotes and some reminders for yourself such as 'Moods are like the weather, they will change', that can comfort and reassure you when you're feeling low. You could add in a compliment someone once gave you, good advice someone has given you, a letter to yourself that you've written when you're feeling OK to read when you're not so OK.
- Childhood comforters: simple items like a teddy, stuffed animal or blanket. If they soothed you when you were young, they will probably do so again.
- Your favourite sweets.

JOURNALLING

When you're going through tough times, you might find it difficult to explain what's happening and how you're feeling to others. If that's the case, writing about it can be helpful and may lead to talking to others and reaching out for support.

Journalling – regularly writing down your thoughts and feelings every day or every few days – can help you to organise those thoughts and feelings. So can writing about a situation after it's happened; it can help your mind to break free of the endless going over and over and reliving a difficult event or period in your life.

In his early 20s, Ollie Aplin experienced a breakdown after living with his mum's years of mental ill health and suicide. While recovering, Ollie's therapist recommended he try journalling as a way to get his feelings out. 'If I couldn't talk, then I could try to write. This realisation was life-changing,' says Ollie. Not only did his journal provide a safe place that helped him to get all his thoughts out of his head, but it helped Ollie express how he was feeling, so that he could talk about it in his therapy sessions and to his dad and his partner. Recognising the benefits of journalling led to Ollie being the co-founder, in 2016, of the 'MindJournal', www.mindjournals.com/

In a 2017 interview with the *Guardian* newspapaper, Ollie said that now he only journals if he's having panic attacks or an anxiety attack. 'If I'm not getting those symptoms, then I don't journal. But I'm also aware of the fact that if I don't journal, I usually end up having more anxious days and more panic attacks.'

The idea that keeping a journal is good for your mental health comes from the work of psychology professor James Pennebaker, at the University of Texas at Austin whose research in the1980s (outlined in his book *Opening Up: The Healing Power of Expressing Emotion*) showed that 'expressive writing' was beneficial for both mental and physical health.

With expressive writing, the idea is that if you're distressed about something, you set aside three to four days to write about your thoughts and feelings for 15 to 20 minutes a day.

Why only write for a short period? In an interview in 2018 in the *New York Times* Dr Pennebaker says that if you're going through a difficult time, writing too much 'becomes more like rumination and that's the last thing in the world you need. My recommendation is to think of expressive writing as a life course correction. As opposed to something you have to commit to doing every day for the rest of your life.'

Whether you write your journal entries by hand, type on a laptop or even on your phone, whichever is more comfortable and convenient for you, the point is simply to get started.

COPING WITH GRIEF

In April 2019 in an article for the *Guardian* newspaper, journalist Vanessa Billy described how in the weeks following her father's death, people offered condolences and gave her space; her work colleagues were supportive, providing back-up, patience and flexibility. A couple of months later, though, Vanessa wrote: 'I still had uncontrollable fits of crying or sadness, only met by uncomfortable silence and awkward looks around me ... Many times, I felt like watching the train I was supposed to be on depart while I stayed stuck on the platform.'

Vanessa did try to get back to her 'normal' self. She tried social-ising but found it difficult to handle simple conversations. 'In-creasingly, I started noticing people's uneasiness if I mentioned how I felt or the memories of my father. I now know that their embarrassment came from not knowing how to react.

I knew grief was going to be painful. What I didn't know was how lonely it would make me feel.'

After a couple of months, Vanessa started to see a grief counsel-lor. 'This decision gave me my life back. The counsellor simply provided me with the space I needed to grieve. We spoke about my dad, about his last days, I cried a lot. Simply talking about it with someone who told me all this was normal gave me im-mense relief.'

Whether you're feeling shocked, **sad, confused or nothing** at all. It's important to allow space for **your feelings and** know that whatever you are or are not feeling, **it's OK.**

Talk about them. Talking to someone – face to face, on the phone or by email or messaging – about your feelings and/or about the other person can be helpful. You may have a family member or friends who will talk and listen to you. You might want to talk to a faith or spiritual leader. Cruse offer support sessions and a helpline for those one-off calls when you just need someone to talk to, www.cruse.org.uk. Their helpline is 0808 808 1677.

Find ways to remember them. When someone dies the memory of them doesn't die; we don't stop relating to the person because they are no longer alive and with us. In different ways, they still live on in us. It can help to think of ways to remember the person who has died and keep them as part of your life. You might have something of theirs that was meaningful to them or meant something special to you about them, that you can keep on display or bring out whenever you feel the need to connect with and remember them. You could create a 'memory box' or an album of photos.

You may want to organise a time each year for family and friends to come together and remember the family member or friend who has died. In fact, because significant dates, like birthdays, anniversaries or other reminders, may be particularly difficult, decide in advance how you want to mark them and let others who are close to you know.

FURTHER SUPPORT AND ADVICE

The UK charity Cruse – who provide support and information for people who have experienced bereavement – recognise that there is no 'right' way to grieve, and everyone experiences bereavement differently.

'However,' says Cruse, 'there are some common feelings that many people share, and these can be painful, surprising or even frightening. As well as shock and numbness, people often feel regret, guilt or anger. We may feel very differently from one moment to the next, and the feelings can often contradict each other. They may come upon us when least expected, which can be confusing and distressing.'

As well as the difficult emotions that come with grief, it's not unusual for grief to affect you in physical ways – headaches or stomach aches, weight loss, sleep disturbance or fatigue. It's also possible to feel that the person who has died is actually present with you. For some people this can be reassuring, but for others it can be upsetting and disturbing.

A bereavement and the experience of grief can affect your relationships with other people; with friends and family members. It can bring people together, but it can also create tension. You may find that significant dates like birthdays, anniversaries and holidays or other reminders can be particularly difficult for you and others who share your loss.

Although it can be incredibly painful at times, **grieving cannot be rushed.**

Whatever you're going through or have experienced – a bereavement, loss of your job, relationship breakup, an injury, a physical or mental illness – even though you may have to be persistent and find the support that's right for you, there is help available; there *will* be support there for you. But you've got to make the first move.

Google a relevant support group and/or helpline. You'll be able to talk to people, people who understand what you're going through, provide opportunities to share experiences and information, ideas on how to move on or feel better. Remember, asking for help doesn't mean you're inadequate, it simply means you need help, support and advice with a specific issue for a time.

Below are just some of the organisations that can be of help.

CRUSE www.cruse.org.uk Cruse provide support and information for people who have experienced bereavement. Their helpline is 0808 808 1677.

The Good Grief Project www.thegoodgriefproject.co.uk/ The Good Grief Project supports families grieving after the untimely death of a loved one, particularly the death of a child.

Mind mind.org.uk Mind provide information and support for anyone experiencing a mental health problem.

The UK Council for Psychotherapy (UKCP) psychotherapy.org.uk/ and **The British Association of Counselling and Psychotherapy** (BACP) bacp.co.uk. UKCP and BACP have details of qualified registered therapists.

Samaritans https://www.samaritans.org/ The Samaritans provide emotional support to anyone in emotional distress, struggling to cope or at risk of suicide. Phone 116 123 or email jo@samaritans.org. Please don't struggle on your own. Do call or email them.

MORE QUOTES FOR COMFORT

'There is nothing like staying at home for real comfort.'
– Jane Austen

'A library is a good place to go when you feel unhappy, for there, in a book, you may find encouragement and comfort.'
– E.B. White

'Cats are connoisseurs of comfort.'
– James Herriot

'Art is to console those who are broken by life.'
– Vincent van Gogh

'Nature is my church. The wind in the trees and the bugs and the frogs. All those things are comfort to me.'
– Sissy Spacek

'Piglet is so small that he slips into a pocket, where it is very comfortable to feel him when you are not quite sure whether twice seven is twelve or twenty-two.'
– A.A. Milne, Winnie-the-Pooh

'Sometimes your joy is the source of your smile, but sometimes your smile can be the source of your joy.'
– Thich Nhat Hanh

'I don't think of all the misery, but of the beauty that still remains.'
— Anne Frank

'Words of comfort, skillfully administered, are the oldest therapy known to man.'
— Louis Nizer

'We find comfort among those who agree with us, growth among those who don't.'
— Frank A. Clark

'There is a comfort in rituals, and rituals provide a framework for stability when you are trying to find answers.'
— Deborah Norville

'Food is a lot of people's therapy – when we say comfort food, we really mean that. It's releasing dopamine and serotonin in your brain that makes you feel good.'
— Brett Hoebel

'Never underestimate how much assistance, how much satisfaction, how much comfort, how much soul and transcendence there might be in a well-made taco and a cold bottle of beer.'
— Tom Robbins

'We must accept finite disappointment, but never lose infinite hope.'
— Martin Luther King, Jr.

'You have to be able to get up and dust yourself off and always be going forward.'
— Rita Moreno

May we not count the Days, but make the Days count.

MY NOTES

About the Author

Gill Hasson has written more than 30 books on the subject of wellbeing for adults and for children; books on emotional intelligence, resilience, mindfulness, overcoming anxiety, happiness and kindness. She also delivers teaching and training for education organisations, voluntary and business organisations and the public sector.

Gill's particular interest and motivation is in helping people to find ways to navigate life's ups and downs; to manage the downs and to benefit from the ups; to build their confidence and realise their potential. You can contact Gill at gillhasson@btinternet.com

About the Illustrator

Eliza Todd is the artist and illustrator behind the brand A Peace of Werk. She is a mixed media artist who licenses her art to brands for stationery and home decor worldwide. Through her brand A Peace of Werk, Eliza strives to create art that is uplifting and encourages us to remember that through all of life's ups and downs there is beauty and richness to be found in the journey. You can follow her on her Instagram page @apeaceofwerk or visit her at www.apeaceofwerk.com

ALSO BY GILL HASSON

In Paperback:

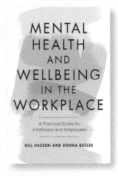

Lonely Less
How to Connect with
Others, Make Friends and
Feel Less Lonely
978-0-85708-904-5

Career Finder
Where to Go from Here
for a Successful Future
978-0-85708-864-2

**Mental Health and
Wellbeing in the
Workplace**
A Practical Guide for
Employers and Employees
978-0-85708-828-4

Productivity
Get Motivated,
Get Organised and
Get Things Done
978-0-85708-784-3

Communication
How to Connect
with Anyone
978-0-85708-750-8

ALSO BY GILL HASSON

In Paperback:

Happiness
How to Get into the
Habit of Being Happy
978-0-85708-759-1

Kindness
Change Your Life
and Make the World a
Kinder Place
978-0-8570-8752-2

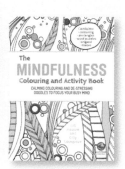

**The Mindfulness Colouring
and Activity Book**
Calming Colouring and
De-stressing Doodles to
Focus Your Busy Mind
978-0-8570-8678-5

Declutter Your Life
How Outer Order Leads
to Inner Calm
978-0-85708-737-9

Emotional Intelligence
Managing Emotions to Make a Positive
Impact on Your Life and Career
978-0-85708-544-3

ALSO BY GILL HASSON

In Paperback:

How to Deal With Difficult People
Smart Tactics for Overcoming the Problem People in Your Life
978-0-85708-567-2

Overcoming Anxiety
Reassuring Ways to Break Free from Stress and Worry and Lead a Calmer Life
978-0-85708-630-3

In Hardback:

The Self-Care Handbook
Connect with Yourself and Boost Your Wellbeing
978-0-85708-812-3

Positive Thinking
Find Happiness and Achieve Your Goals Through the Power of Positive Thought
978-0-85708-683-9

Mindfulness
Be Mindful. Live in the Moment
978-0-85708-444-6

ALSO BY GILL HASSON

Pocketbook Series:

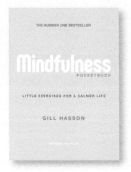

Mindfulness Pocketbook
Little Exercises for a Calmer
Life, 2nd Edition
978-0-85708-872-7

**Positive Thinking
Pocketbook**
Little Exercises for a Happy
and Successful Life
978-0-85708-754-6

Confidence Pocketbook
Little Exercises for a
Self-Assured Life
978-0-85708-733-1

**Emotional Intelligence
Pocketbook**
Little Exercises for an
Intuitive Life
978-0-85708-730-0